MACMILLAN CULTURAL READERS
INTERMEDIATE LEVEL

W0099626

JENNIFER GASCOIGNE

China

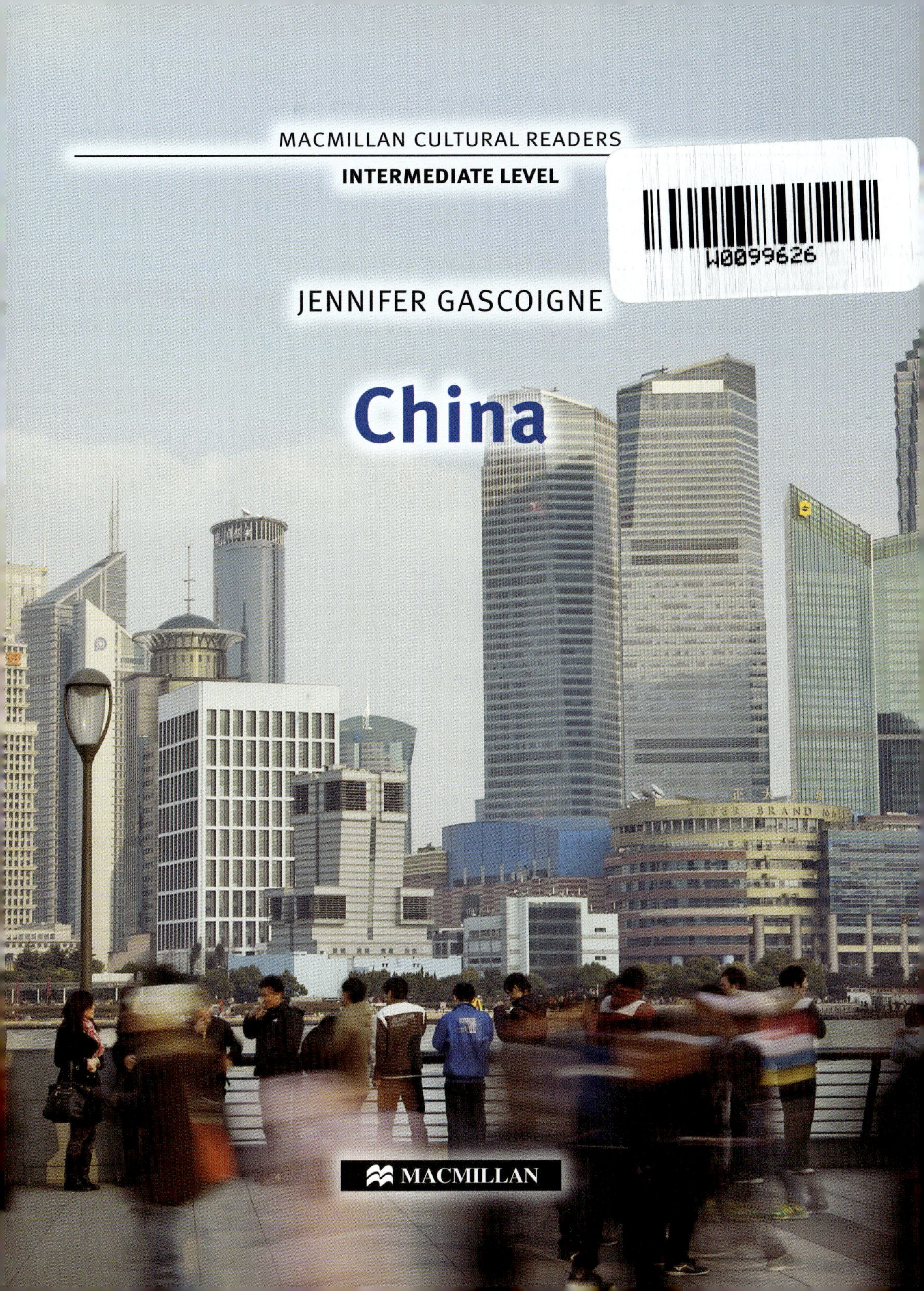

MACMILLAN

INTERMEDIATE LEVEL

Founding Editor of the Macmillan Readers: John Milne

The Macmillan Readers provide a choice of enjoyable reading materials for learners of English. The series is published at six levels – Starter, Beginner, Elementary, Pre-intermediate, Intermediate and Upper. The Macmillan Cultural Readers are a factual strand of the series.

Level Control

Information, structure and vocabulary are controlled to suit the students' ability at each level.

The number of words at each level:

Starter	about 300 basic words
Beginner	about 600 basic words
Elementary	about 1100 basic words
Pre-intermediate	about 1400 basic words
Intermediate	about 1600 basic words
Upper	about 2200 basic words

Vocabulary

Some difficult words and phrases in this book are important for understanding the text. Some of these words are explained in the text, some are shown in the pictures and others are marked with a number like this: [3]. Phrases are marked with [P]. Words with a number are explained in the *Glossary* at the end of the book and phrases are explained on the *Useful Phrases* page.

Answer Keys

Answer Keys for the *Points For Understanding* and *Exercises* sections can be found at www.macmillanenglish.com/readers.

Audio Download

There is an audio download available to buy for this title. Visit www.macmillanenglish.com/readers for more information.

Contents

The Places In The Book

N

KAZAKHSTAN

KYRGYZSTAN

Urumqi

UZBEKISTAN

TAJIKISTAN

XINJIANG

TURKMENISTAN

AFGHANISTAN

PAKISTAN

TIBET

NEPAL

Lhasa

BHUTAN

KEY

Autonomous Regions: areas that have their own local government[1] and can also make some laws

Provinces: areas with their own local government

Municipalities: cities with their own local government

Special Administrative Regions: areas that have their own local government and can make their own laws

BANGLADESH

INDIA

MYANMA

INDIAN OCEAN

RUSSIA

MONGOLIA

HEILONGJIANG
• Harbin

Changchun •
JILIN

Shenyang •
LIAONING

NORTH
KOREA

SOUTH
KOREA

Hohhot •
INNER MONGOLIA

BEIJING
HEBEI   • Tianjin

Yinchuan •
NINGXIA

Taiyuan •
Shijiazhuang •
SHANXI

Jining •
SHANDONG

Xining •   Lanzhou •
QINGHAI   GANSU

Xi'an •
SHAANXI

Zhengzhou •
HENAN

JIANGSU

Hefei •   Nanjing •
SHANGHAI

CHINA

HUBEI

ANHUI

Chengdu •

Wuhan •

Hangzhou •

SICHUAN

Chongquing •
CHONGQUING

Changsha •

Nanchang •

ZHEJIANG

PACIFIC
OCEAN

HUNAN

JIANGXI

GUIZHOU

Fuzhou •
FUJIAN

Guiyang •

Kunming •

TAIWAN

YUNNAN

GUANGXI

GUANGDONG
• Guangzhou

Nanning •

HONG KONG

MACAU

VIETNAM

LAOS

THAILAND

5

Welcome to China

China is the world's third biggest country and the country with the largest population—the most people living there. Most people live in the east, near the coast. Most Chinese people speak Mandarin but some ethnic minority groups[2] speak different languages.

It is a country of many different landscapes[3]: high mountains, deserts, grasslands, big rivers, forests and some of the biggest cities in the world. It is famous for its culture, its food and, of course, its wall – the Great Wall of China.

The country has a very long history – more than 4,000 years – which makes it one of the world's oldest civilizations[4]. From around 1600 BC until the beginning of the twentieth century it was ruled by emperors[5], who gave their names to the period of time they ruled. These periods are called dynasties and the last dynasty ended in 1911. After that, China became a republic and was governed by a president. Then, in 1949, the Communist party with Mao Zedong as its leader took control[P]. He gave the country a new name – the People's Republic of China (PRC). During this period, the government (or state) controlled everything, and everyone in the PRC worked for the state.

Since the end of the twentieth century, China has been changing very fast. Today it is an important centre for industry and makes many of the things we use in our daily lives: clothes, shoes, televisions and computers are only a few. China has become a rich country and now has one of the strongest economies[6] in the world.

The flag of the People's Republic of China is red with a large yellow star that represents the Communist Party of China and four smaller stars that represent the four social classes[7]. The colour red represents revolution[8].

Warm-up quiz

1 What is a yak?
- **a** a language
- **b** an animal
- **c** a building
- **d** a fruit

2 Which colour is the name of a big river in China?
- **a** Red
- **b** Black
- **c** White
- **d** Yellow

3 Which material has given its name to roads connecting the East and West?
- **a** cotton
- **b** wool
- **c** silk
- **d** paper

4 Who did Hong Kong belong to until 1997?
- **a** the British
- **b** the Portuguese
- **c** the Japanese
- **d** the Dutch

5 Where did Ghenghis Khan come from?
- **a** Siberia
- **b** Thailand
- **c** Manchuria
- **d** Mongolia

6 Who was Bruce Lee?
- **a** an actor
- **b** a writer
- **c** an artist
- **d** a politician

7 What is the name of the long pasta eaten in China?
- **a** spaghetti
- **b** rice
- **c** noodles
- **d** bamboo

8 Which is the most important holiday in China?
- **a** Christmas
- **b** New Year
- **c** Mid-Autumn Festival
- **d** National Day

9 What was the symbol[9] of the Chinese emperors?
- **a** a dragon
- **b** a lion
- **c** an elephant
- **d** a snake

10 In which year were the Olympic Games™ held in China?
- **a** 2000
- **b** 2004
- **c** 2008
- **d** 2012

1 The Land, the People and the Language

Longji terrace

China covers a large geographical area so it is a country with many different landscapes. There are high mountains and plateaus[10] in the south-west, dry sandy deserts in the north and north-west, large areas of grasslands and forests in the north-east and forests, and huge river deltas and fertile lowlands near the coast in the east and the south. Its size and the big differences in the height of the land mean that the climate from north to south and east to west changes a lot, too.

In the north, summers are very hot and dry but winters are very cold and temperatures can go as low as -41°C in some places. Strong winds in winter and spring blow large clouds of sand from the deserts towards the north-east coast. In cities like the capital Beijing, the sand clouds are often so thick that it is difficult for people to see. In central China summers are long, hot and humid[11] and winters are short, wet and cold. The high plateaus in the south-west have very cold winters but little rain but the lowlands in the south-east are wet and warm all of the year.

> The name 'China' probably comes from the name of the Qin Emperors (221–206 BC), who were the first emperors to rule over all of China. The Chinese people call their country *Zhōngguó*, which means 'Middle Country'.

The Land, the People and the Language

Geography

The Tibetan Plateau in the south-west is over 4,000 metres above the sea and is often called the 'roof of the world'. There are high mountains all around it. The highest mountain in the world, Mount Everest (8,850 metres), is in the Himalayas on the China–Nepal border[12].

> Mount Everest was named after Sir George Everest, who was the first person to describe exactly where it was and how high it was. The Chinese call it *Mount Zhumulangma*.

It is too cold and dry to grow anything on the plateau so the local people keep animals like yaks and sheep. Yaks are very important for the Tibetan

A yak

people. They use their hair to make clothes and tents and their skin to make boots and boats. They eat yak meat and drink yak milk. Tibetans are nomads – people who travel from place to place, and live in tents. In the lower valleys of the plateau farmers can grow crops and vegetables.

The Taklamakan Desert in the north-west of China is the largest sandy desert in the world. There is almost no water and very little plant and animal life, so people do not live there. Until the beginning of the twentieth century, tigers[13] could still be found in the desert. There are still some wild camels[14] but they are disappearing fast.

Another desert in the north, **the Gobi Desert,** is famous in history because the old trade[15] routes known as the Silk Road cross the southern part of it.

In north-central China, **the Loess Plateau** is home to more than fifty million people. It is called the Loess Plateau because of the yellow soil (*loess*) which is found all over the plateau. It was once a rich and fertile place, covered in forests and grasslands, but over thousands of years the land became dry because of bad farming methods. Today, however, thanks to a large development project[16], farmers are again growing enough food to feed themselves and their families.

> The old *Silk Road* joined Asia, Europe and parts of Africa. It gets its name from the Chinese silk trade that began in the Han dynasty (206 BC to AD 220). Marco Polo described it in his book *Travels of Marco Polo* about his journey across northern China.

The two great rivers of China, the Yangtze (6,418 kilometres) and the Yellow River (5,464 kilometres) start on the Tibetan Plateau in the west and flow down to the East China Sea.

Several times in the history of China, the Yangtze was a dividing line between the north and the south. People have lived on the land along it for thousands of years and much of the country's food comes from the river valley. As well as being politically and economically important, the Yangtze has great cultural meaning too. It flows through one of China's most beautiful natural landscapes – the Three Gorges in Chongqing Municipality and Hubei province. For centuries its deep valleys and high mountains have inspired[17] Chinese poets and artists.

The Three Gorges valley is a popular place to visit by boat.

The Yellow River gets its name and colour from the yellow soil it picks up as it flows through the Loess Plateau. The Chinese people call it 'the Mother River' because its basin was the birthplace[18] of ancient Chinese culture. It is also called 'the river of sorrow[19]' because millions of people have died in the terrible floods that happen when there is too much loess in it. The worst flood was in 1931 when more than one million people died.

The third longest river in China is the Pearl River (2,400 kilometers). Its delta on the South China Sea is a very densely populated area – around forty-six million people live there. It is often called the workshop[20] of China because of all the factories that are there. It is the fastest-growing and richest area in the country.

- In 2011 work began on the 30 kilometre Hong Kong – Zhuhai – Macau Bridge (HZMB) across the Pearl River. It will be the longest man-made sea-crossing in the world.

Government

China, or the People's Republic of China (PRC), became a communist country in 1949. With over eighty million members, the Chinese Communist Party is the largest political party in the world.

The country is divided into twenty-two provinces, four municipalities or cities with their own government, five Autonomous Regions and two Special Administrative Regions. You can see these areas on the map on page 5.

The Autonomous Regions each have large numbers of a particular ethnic minority:
- Xinjiang (Uyghur people)
- Ningxia (Hui people)
- Inner Mongolia (Mongols)
- Guangxi (Zhuang people)
- Tibet (Tibetans)

The Special Administrative Region of Hong Kong was given to Britain by China in 1842 after a war. On 1st July 1997, Britain gave it back and it became part of the PRC. After that, large numbers of people from other parts of the PRC went there to look for work. They found jobs in factories and Hong Kong developed into an important financial centre. There are about 260 islands in Hong Kong. The largest is Lantau Island. The second largest is Hong Kong Island.

Macau was governed by Portugal for 442 years until 20th December 1999. It was the first place in East Asia where Europeans made their homes.

The people of China

There are fifty-six different ethnic groups in China. Most of them have their own beliefs[21] and customs, and sometimes their own language. Many still wear traditional clothes, some of which are very beautiful. Tourists from China as well as from other countries like to visit the areas where ethnic groups live to see these traditional clothes and the way the people there live.

The largest ethnic group is **the Han**. About ninety-two percent of the population of China are Han. They are also the largest ethnic group in the world – about twenty percent (1.3 billion) of all the people in the world are Han. In the English-speaking world they are often known as simply 'Chinese'. The name Han comes from the Han dynasty (206 BC to AD 220), the longest-ruling dynasty in Chinese history.

The largest ethnic minority group is **the Zhuang** (over sixteen million people) who live mainly in the Guanxi Zhuang Autonomous Region in the south. The Zhuang language belongs to the Chinese-Tibetan language family but they use Roman letters and not Chinese characters for their writing system[22]. In China the Zhuang are known for their love of singing and their beautiful silk brocade.

The Uyghur (about eight million people) is another large ethnic minority group. They live in the Xinjiang Uyghur Autonomous Region in the north-west of the country. Their language is like Turkish and most of them are Muslim (of Islamic religion). They, too, love music and play many different kinds of instruments. They are famous for the *muqam*, a show with traditional folk songs, dances and poetry that everybody in the village joins in with during local festivals.

Brocade on Zhuang clothes

The Land, the People and the Language

The Manchus are from the Manchurian region of North East Asia. They have their own language but out of the nearly ten million ethnic Manchus in China today, fewer than one hundred, maybe only twenty people, speak it. The last emperor of China – Pu Yi (1906–1967) of the Qing dynasty – was Manchu.

Most of **the Hui** people (nearly ten million) live in the Ningxia Hui Autonomous Region in north-west China. Like the Uyghur, they are Muslim.

The large areas of grassland of the northern Autonomous Region of Inner Mongolia are home to **the Mongols** (about seven million people). They are mainly farmers now but in the past they were nomadic. They followed their camels, cows, horses and sheep across the grasslands on horseback and lived in yurts, Mongolian tents. Yurts are made of strong cotton cloth and felt. Felt is a material made from wool or the fur of animals. Inside the yurt it is warm and comfortable. There is a stove for cooking in the centre and a place at the back of the yurt for older people and guests to sit in.

> **i**
> The great Mongol leader, Ghenghis Khan (AD 1162? – 1227), ruled over an empire that covered most of Asia. His grandson, Kublai Khan (AD 1215–1294), became the ruler of China and started the Yuan dynasty (AD 1279–1368).

The Miao (about nine million people) are one of the largest ethnic minorities in south-west China. They live mainly in the hilly regions of Guizhou, Yunnan, Hunan and Sichuan provinces and the Guangxi Zhuang Autonomous Region. Their language belongs to the Chinese–Tibetan family of languages and there are many different varieties. However, it is disappearing fast because the Miao are using Mandarin Chinese instead.

The Chinese language

Chinese written words look very different to those of other languages. They are based on simple drawings for important words and ideas, such as 'man', 'horse' or 'water'. The earliest drawings, or characters, are very old and were first seen in 1400 BC. Over the years, more lines were added to make new words and most Chinese characters are made up of[P] different meanings and sounds. Chinese dictionaries may contain more than forty thousand of these characters and each character usually has several meanings. This makes Chinese very difficult to learn and before the 1950s around eighty percent of Chinese people could not read or write. Since then, the number has fallen to less than ten percent thanks to education, the introduction of easier forms of Chinese characters and *pinyin*, a way of writing Chinese in Roman script. There are about 6,500 easier characters. However, you only need to know about 3,000 of them to read a newspaper in China.

There are many different forms of spoken Chinese. The most common ones are Mandarin, Cantonese and Wu. Chinese is a tonal language, which means the pitch (the high or low quality of a sound) can change the meaning. For example, the word for 'soup' and 'sugar' is the same – *tang*. But if you say it with a high tone, it means 'soup' and with a rising tone, it means 'sugar'.

- Mandarin – spoken in Beijing and the official[23] spoken language in the PRC.
- Cantonese – spoken in Hong Kong, Macau, Guandong Province and south-east Guangxi Province
- Wu – spoken in Shanghai, Zhenjiang Province and southern Jiangsu Province

2 The Dynasties

The Terracotta Army

Dynasties in China were periods during which an Emperor and his family ruled the country. There were more than thirty dynasties in Chinese history, from the first Xia dynasty (about 2205–1766 BC) to the last dynasty, the Qing (AD 1644–1911).

The Qin dynasty (221–206 BC)

This was the first dynasty to rule all of China. The first emperor, Qin Shi-huang, ruled for nine years and did many good things. He reorganized the government, built roads, canals and palaces and made Chinese writing easier.

He also built a wall along the northern border of the new empire to keep out his enemies. This was the first part of the Great Wall of China. In 215 BC work began on the Emperor's tomb – the place where his body would go when he died. It was the size of a city and was the biggest tomb ever built in China. It contained everything the Emperor might need for his life after he died, including an army of terracotta (clay[24]) soldiers that were the size of real people. They were found in 1974 and so far archeologists[25] have saved two thousand of them, but they think that there may be over eight thousand, as well as clay horses and chariots[26].

The Han dynasty (206 BC–AD 220)

This four-hundred-year period was a time of order and prosperity[27] in China and is sometimes called China's first 'golden age'. There was great technological and scientific progress. Paper and printing[28] methods, water clocks for telling the time and many scientific instruments were all invented during the Han dynasty. The Empire got bigger and trade with the West became easier thanks to the Silk Road. In the first century AD, Buddhism was brought to China from India by traders along the Silk Road.

Poetry, literature and philosophy increased[29] with the invention of paper. The first history of China, *Shiji* (Historical Records), written by Sima Qian (145-86 BC), became the model for later books on Chinese history. It contains descriptions of emperors, dynasties and important people from 2600 BC, the time of the legendary[30] emperor Huangdi, called the Yellow Emperor, to 93 BC.

Confucianism, a system of ideas based on the teachings of the philosopher Confucius (551–479 BC), became China's official political philosophy

under Emperor Wudi, who ruled from 141 to 87 BC. He opened an imperial university where people who wanted to work for the government had to remember the 431,286 words of the ancient Confucian texts. In 124 BC, he introduced examinations for people who worked for the government. This was good for the country because it meant that only the best people got the jobs. Before that the emperors had given all the important positions to their favourite people even if they were not the best. Strong leaders like Wudi made China in the Han dynasty one of the most powerful countries in the world for hundreds of years.

Confucius

Confucius was a teacher and philosopher. He was born in a city near Qufu in modern Shandong Province. Historians are not sure if he wrote any books himself, but his ideas were recorded by his students in a book known as the *Analects*.

Confucius believed that rulers should be a good example for their people, and the people should respect their rulers and do what they told them.

The Period of Disunity (220–589)

The Han dynasty ended in AD 220 and three-and-a-half centuries of war and fighting followed. It was the longest period of disunity (when China was not one united country) in Chinese history.

In 317 non-Han people from Mongolia and Manchuria conquered[31] the north of the country and became the new rulers. They were known as the Northern Dynasties. They were happy to accept the Chinese way of life: they wore Chinese clothes, used Chinese writing and many of them married Chinese people. They also changed their religion and became Buddhists. Their rulers learnt Chinese and changed their name to a Chinese name – Yuan.

Because of all the fighting in the north, many Han Chinese escaped to the south, where Chinese emperors continued to rule. They were known as the Southern Dynasties.

Then in 577 the northern rulers conquered the southern states and China was once again united as one country. Four years later, a soldier called Yang Jian started the Sui dynasty.

During this period of war and disunity, Buddhism and Daoism, an ancient philosophy that is also a religion, became very popular. Perhaps people were looking for an escape from the fighting or perhaps they were attracted by the promise of life after death that both religions offered. Religion brought people together again after many years of fighting and being ruled by many different rulers.

Daoism, or Taoism, developed from ancient beliefs based on the writings of two philosophers, Laozi (sixth century BC) and Zhuangzi (fourth century BC). The word *dao* means 'the way'. For Laozi it was the way taken by nature. He thought people should live simple lives and follow the *dao*, in other words, accept the forces[32] of nature. By doing this they could become immortal – they would never die.

17

The Sui dynasty (589–618) and the Tang dynasty (618–907)

Yang Jian, known as Wendi, ruled for 23 years and was a good, strong emperor. He is most famous for building a long canal system that linked the Yellow River and the Yangtzi. It is still the longest canal in the world (1,800 kilometres long).

After Wendi's death, his son Yangdi ruled for thirteen years. He was a bad ruler, however, and the people rebelled[33]. In the end, Yangdi was killed by a government official, Li Yuan, who became the first Emperor of the Tang dynasty.

One of the greatest emperors in Chinese history was the second Tang Emperor, Taizong, who ruled from 626 to 649. China had a period of peace and prosperity under his rule that continued for more than a century after his death.

During the thousands of years of imperial Chinese history, there was only one female Emperor (Empress) – Wu Zetian, who ruled from 690 to 705. She was Taizong's favourite wife and a very intelligent and beautiful woman. He made her his secretary and always asked for her advice before he made important decisions.

Wu was only twenty-seven years old when Taizong died. The new Emperor, Gaozong, liked Wu and he married her. He was a weak man, however, and he became ill, so Wu ruled the country for him. After he died, she became Empress.

Empress Wu was a good ruler. She was a Buddhist and Buddhist culture grew under her rule. She built many temples[34], which became important centres for teaching Buddhism and for creating Buddhist art.

The Northern Song (960–1126) and Southern Song (1127–1279) dynasties

960	1126	1232	1234	1279	i
A military officer called Zhao founded[35] the Song dynasty (known later as the Northern Song).	The Jin dynasty from Manchuria defeated[36] the Song. The Song Emperor was forced to escape to the south (the Southern Song).	The Mongols and Southern Song defeated the Jin.	The Jin Emperor died and the north became part of the Mongol Empire.	The Mongols under Kublai Khan, Ghenghis Khan's grandson, conquered the Southern Song.	

The Song dynasty was another golden age in Chinese history. China was probably the richest country in the world and technologically and culturally ahead of the West. Inventions like movable type printing meant that many more books could be printed and, so, were cheaper to buy. As a result, the number of educated people increased.

Moveable type printing was invented between 1045 and 1058 by a man named Bi Sheng. Before that, pages of books were printed using one piece of wood. It was expensive and took a long time. Bi Sheng took small pieces of clay and wrote a character on each one so that the pieces could be used many times to make different texts. It was an important development in the history of printing.

During the Song dynasty, paper money was used for the first time and factories employing thousands of people were built to make it. Towns and cities became much bigger. Trade with other countries also increased. The invention of the compass made it easier for people to cross the seas and travel to Southeast Asia and begin new trade there.

The Chinese invented the compass.

The Yuan dynasty (1279–1368)

In 1279, the Mongol leader Kublai Khan became Emperor of the Yuan dynasty, the first non-Han dynasty to rule all of China. However, the Mongol rulers were not popular with the Chinese people because they gave the best jobs in the government to their people. In the 1350s there were rebellions and Yuan rule began to fail. Then, in 1368, Zhu Yuanzhang, a Buddhist monk[37], defeated the Mongols and became the first Emperor of the Ming dynasty.

The Ming dynasty (1368–1644)

The third Ming Emperor, the Yongle Emperor, who ruled from 1402 to 1424, made Beijing the capital city and built a large palace for himself and his family there. It was called the Forbidden City and it was also the centre of government. The Yongle Emperor was interested in the world outside China so he built some very big ships and sent his friend Zheng He to explore countries across the seas.

Zheng He made six long trips to Southeast Asia, India, the Middle East and Africa between 1403 and 1419 in 300 very big ships that carried nearly 30,000 men. The largest of his ships was longer than a football field. He brought back many animals from his trips to Africa, including a giraffe.

The thirteenth Emperor, Wanli, made the Great Wall stronger and longer. Emperors after Wanli also continued to add to the Wall. The building work cost so much money that there was very little money left to spend when the seventeenth and last Emperor, the Chongzhen Emperor (1611–1644), started to rule. The country had other problems at that time too. The Manchus were attacking the northern border and the people in the countryside were rebelling because the harvests[38] had been bad and they did not have enough to eat. In the end the Manchus broke through the Great Wall and conquered Beijing. The Chongzhen Emperor killed himself and the Manchus made a five-year-old boy the first Emperor of the Qing dynasty. The boy's name was Shunzhi.

The Qing dynasty (1644–1911)

The Manchus did not know how to govern a country as big as China so they decided to continue using Chinese methods of government. Offices in the capital had both a Chinese and a Manchu boss and government officials still had to do the traditional examinations that were based on knowing the ideas of Confucius.

Although the Manchu emperors did not make many changes to the way the country was governed, they kept their own culture. They continued to speak Manchu, for example, and, to show their power over the Han, they made all men wear their hair in a pigtail style called the Manchu 'queue'.

At first there was prosperity in China under Qing rule but it slowly started to become weaker during the second half of the nineteenth century and the early years of the twentieth century. This was because of problems inside and outside

A Manchu queue

the country. During the eighteenth century, several European countries became very interested in trading with China. The United Kingdom was interested in buying silk and tea, for example. After the first Anglo–Chinese War (1839–1842), China had to agree to open several Chinese ports[39] to foreign trade and to give Hong Kong to Britain. After another war (1856), Britain, France and Russia won a lot more control over China and the Han Chinese began to think that the Qing were not governing well. A change was needed. In 1900 there was a rebellion. The rebels were defeated, however, by an international army of 2,100 American, British, Russian, French, Italian, German, Austro–Hungarian and Japanese soldiers. The end of the Qing dynasty finally came in 1911. After more than four thousand years of being ruled by emperors, China became a republic.

> - Like the Ming, the Qing emperors and their families lived in the Forbidden City.
> - It is called the Forbidden City because ordinary people were not allowed inside its gates.
> - The City is said to have 9,999 rooms (nine is a lucky number in China).
> - It was opened to the public in 1925 and today it is used as a museum.

3 Chinese Art

A traditional Chinese painting

Chinese art has a history of more than five thousand years. The most developed art forms are porcelain (objects made of a special white clay), calligraphy (artistic writing) and paintings done in ink[40] of landscapes, birds and flowers. The earliest Chinese art objects were found in tombs and include ceramics (objects made of clay) like the terracotta army of the Qin dynasty.

Porcelain

Although porcelain was probably invented in the second century AD, it was during the Sui dynasty (581–618) that really beautiful porcelain objects started to be made. In the fifteenth century, traders who travelled the Silk Road began taking porcelain to Europe to sell, where it became extremely popular. By the sixteenth century, the Europeans could not get enough of it[P] and porcelain became so expensive that people called it 'white gold'. The Portuguese began trading with the Ming dynasty in 1517 and the Dutch followed in 1598. This trade continued until the middle of the seventeenth century when civil wars[41] caused the end of the Ming dynasty in 1644. Soon after that, in 1708, the Germans discovered the recipe for making porcelain, which the Chinese had kept secret for nearly one thousand years.

Most Chinese porcelain was, and still is, made in the city of Jingdezhen in southern China. For many centuries, this city was able to make all the porcelain Asia, Europe and America wanted. For this reason, it is known as 'the capital of porcelain'.

Tang sancai

'Sancai' means three colours and the glaze[42] on this porcelain is typically green, yellow and white/cream. Tang sancai objects were made for the tombs of rich Tang people and are usually in the form of people and animals from daily life.

Longquan celadon

The term 'celadon' is used to describe porcelain with a blue-green glaze. It is also the name of the glaze. The finest celadons were made at kilns in the Longquan area of southern Zhejiang province during the Song dynasty.

Blue and white

Cobalt blue, the blue used to decorate[43] the blue and white porcelain, probably came to China from the Middle East as early as the ninth century. Blue and white porcelain first appeared during the Yuan dynasty (1127–1279), but it was during the Ming dynasty (1368–1644) that it became really popular.

Calligraphy

The Chinese written language began to develop more than three thousand years ago. There are five basic types of writing, including one type that is used only for writing notes.

The English word 'calligraphy' means 'beautiful writing'. The Chinese name for calligraphy is *Shūfǎ*, which means 'the way of writing'. But calligraphy is more than a way of writing – it is an art form like painting. The two arts, in fact, developed at the same time and both used brushes and ink. Until the Song period, however, calligraphy was thought of as a more important form of art than painting, and calligraphy written on silk was hung on walls like paintings.

The calligrapher uses brushes, paper, inksticks and an inkstone – a stone on which he makes the ink with water. These are known as 'The Four Treasures of the Study'.

For serious calligraphers, the inkstone is as important as the kind of ink they use. In ancient China famous artists and calligraphers often gave beautiful decorated inkstones to people as presents. These old inkstones are very valuable today.

> 66 *The writing stops but the meaning goes on; the brush has been put down but the power is unending.* 99
>
> **Chinese saying**

In ancient times, both writing and painting were done on silk. But after the invention of paper in the first century AD, calligraphy artists changed to this newer and cheaper material.

Paper was invented in AD 105 by a court official called Cai Lun. The first country in Europe to produce paper was Spain – nearly one thousand years later!

Many people believe that Xuan paper, produced in Jing County, Anhui Province, is the best paper for Chinese calligraphy. It is soft and easy to write and paint on. It is often called 'rice paper', but it doesn't really contain any rice!

Today people learn calligraphy at school and calligraphy clubs are popular in all regions of China. A lot of practice is needed to become a good calligrapher because it is more difficult to write with a brush than with a pen. Students start with the eight main strokes (lines made with a pen or brush) that form Chinese characters. The strokes must be written in the correct order.

'As a Chinese person, how you write shows who you are. There is a saying that says if you love China you must love Chinese characters because they are so full of meaning, so I feel that a Chinese person must be able to write well.'

CHEN XIAOKANG – A CALLIGRAPHY TEACHER

At the beginning of the 1990s in Beijing, many people started practising calligraphy in public places like streets and parks using very large brushes. They used water as their ink and the ground as their paper. Soon there were water calligraphy artists in most of China's larger cities. Their art work does not last[44] long, only until the water dries, but it is a good way for them to use their calligraphic skills[45] and show other people their art.

Water calligraphy

3

Painting

From the Han to the Tang Dynasties (206 BC–AD 960) the main subjects of Chinese paintings were people at the royal court (the royal palace and everyone who lived and worked there) and animals, especially horses. Horse riding was popular and even the court ladies rode. Some of these ancient paintings, done on pottery[46], silk and walls, can still be seen in tombs.

In the late Tang period, artists started to paint landscapes. Two styles developed: the gold and blue–green landscapes, which had many details, and a one-colour style, which only gave an idea of forms. A landscape was a good subject for a painting, artists thought, because the countryside was beautiful and quiet, and life there was simple. When people looked at a painting of the countryside, it was like being there and made them feel happy.

During the Song period (960–1279), the Emperor opened a royal painting academy – a school for professional painters. Many of them worked for the Emperor and were told what to paint. Large landscapes with lots of colours and details, and pictures of birds with flowers were especially popular with the Southern Song Emperors. In the late Song period the first 'literati' paintings started to appear. The literati were government officials or rich men with a lot of free time. Their paintings were very different from those of the professional painters because they did not paint for money but as a hobby. This meant that they could paint what they wanted to and what they thought was beautiful. They used ink, like the calligraphers, and very few colours, sometimes only one. Their favourite subjects were details of landscapes – bamboo[48], trees, flowers and rocks.

- The Chinese character for 'landscape' has two parts. They mean 'mountains and water'.
- Landscape painting is linked with the philosophy of Daoism, which taught people to live in harmony[47] with the natural world.
- Chinese artists do not usually paint real places but better places that they imagine.

During and after the Yuan period (1279–1368), most educated people thought that the literati paintings were the best, and they started to buy lots of them. They preferred them to the royal academy paintings because the Yuan literati painted not what they saw but what was in their hearts and minds.

Shen Zhou (1427–1509), one of the most famous Ming literati, was a member of a group called the Wu School. For Wu painters, painting was a way to think about something carefully and not a job. For Shen Zhou, a painting was not an object to sell but part of the painter himself.

During the Qing period (1644–1911), two schools of painting developed – one group of painters based its work on the masters[49] of the Yuan period and the other group, known as the individualists, did a freer form of painting.

Art today

Today, Chinese artists use painting, film, video, photography and performance[50] to create their art. Song Dong (born 1966, Beijing) is one of them. In 1995, he began one artwork for which he wrote a daily diary on a flat piece of stone using water. As the water dried, the letters disappeared. Another of his works, called *Eating the City*, is made of food. More recently, he created an artwork called *Waste Not*, which was a collection of over ten thousand things from the home of his mother, who kept everything that could possibly be reused.

Literati painting *Waiting to Cross a River in Autumn* by Zhang Lu

4 Martial Arts

A boy performing martial arts

The martial arts are systems and traditions of fighting. According to a legend, Huangdi, the Yellow Emperor, introduced the earliest fighting systems to China nearly four thousand years ago. He was a famous general who, before becoming China's leader, wrote books about medicine, the stars and martial arts. He developed *jiao di*, a form of fighting which his soldiers used against their enemies in wars. However, the first time martial arts are written about is in a book from the fifth century BC. Since then, hundreds of different fighting styles have developed, each with its own techniques[51]. Many styles copy the way animals move and others are inspired by Chinese philosophies, religions and legends. There are many groups, or schools, of styles. For example, internal styles use and improve[52] mental[53] skills; external styles make the body stronger. Northern styles use kicking movements and Southern styles use short, powerful movements with the arms and the whole body.

Shaolin Temple and Shaolin kung fu

Shaolin Temple on Shaoshi Mountain in Henan province, northern China, is famous for its Buddhist fighting monks and their fighting style, usually known as Shaolin kung fu.

During the Period of Disunity, the emperors of the Northern Wei dynasty (386–534/535) made Buddhism the official state religion. They built hundreds of monasteries (buildings where monks live) and temples, including some in caves[54]. Buddhist monks from India were often invited to come and teach in the temples. One of them, whose name was Batuo, arrived in China around the middle of the fifth century and the Emperor built Shaolin Temple especially for him.

In a traditional legend, an Indian Buddhist monk called Bodhidharma visited Shaolin around the middle of the sixth century. He gave the monks lessons in meditation[55] but he found that they kept falling asleep. In fact, they were very thin, weak and unhealthy because they had to study so much. So, to make them stronger both physically and mentally, Bodhidharma decided to use some exercises in his daily lessons. After many years of exercises the monks were so strong and good at fighting that they were able to protect themselves from the criminals who often came to rob the temple.

When the Northern Wei dynasty ended, the new rulers thought that the temples had become too rich and powerful so they destroyed[56] many of them, and possibly Shaolin too. Later, during the Sui and Tang dynasties, Buddhism became popular again and the temples were rebuilt.

There is a description written on a large stone from the year 728 of two times when the Shaolin fighting monks used their skills outside the temple. The first was in about 610 when they fought some criminals who were attacking the monastery, and the second was when thirteen monks from the temple helped the Tang army to win a battle against the Sui army in 621. To thank them, Emperor Taizong, who admired their amazing fighting skills, gave them some land

> Old stories say that Bodhidharma spent nine years meditating in a cave. He fell asleep only once and was so angry with himself that he cut off his eyelids – the pieces of skin that cover your eyes when they are closed – to stop it from happening again! Where his eyelids hit the floor, tea plants started to grow. Since then, monks have drunk tea to help them to stay awake during meditation.

for the monastery. He also allowed them to continue to be fighting monks and to eat meat (Buddhists do not usually eat meat).

Shaolin monks show their fighting skills.

During the Ming dynasty (1368–1644), monasteries developed into something like universities and the number of fighting monks at Shaolin increased to more than one thousand. The Ming Emperors gave money to the temples and often asked the monks for help to fight rebellions. It was a golden age for Shaolin Temple.

However, in 1644 the Manchus won a battle against the Ming and there was a new dynasty called Qing (1644–1911). The Qing burnt down the Shaolin temples because Ming rebels went there to hide, so the monks had to escape. Some people say they went south and started the Southern Shaolin Monastery in Fujian Province.

Although the temples were gradually rebuilt, the best days were over. Shaolin was destroyed again in 1928 in a fire that lasted for more than forty days. As well as the buildings, valuable books and records on martial arts were lost.

In the 1970s and 1980s, when kung fu films became popular, the Chinese government rebuilt many of the old buildings at Shaolin Temple. Today, students, both Chinese and foreign, study traditional kung fu techniques, Buddhism, Chinese traditional medicine, calligraphy and the Chinese language there. It is also popular with tourists.

The actor Bruce Lee is probably the most important martial artist in history because he introduced Chinese martial arts to the rest of the world. In just a few years, he made millions of people interested in doing martial arts. His film *Enter the Dragon* (1973) made him famous. Unfortunately, he died six days before the film appeared in cinemas.

The Chinese–American martial arts actor, Bruce Lee

Wuxia literature and cinema

The word *wuxia* means 'martial arts hero' and today refers to a particular kind of Chinese literature and cinema that is popular in all Chinese-speaking areas. It became better known internationally when films like Ang Lee's *Crouching Tiger, Hidden Dragon* (2000) and Zhang Yimou's *Hero* (2002) and *House of Flying Daggers* (2004) appeared. The comedy film *Kung Fu Panda* (2008) is an American example of this type of cinema. Although it was not made in China, it was well received by Chinese cinema-goers, who thought it showed a good understanding of their culture.

The *wuxia* novel began in the early twentieth century – the films, TV series and video games came much later. The stories are adventure stories that often take place in the ancient past. They have some things in common with Japanese and medieval[57] European stories of knights, but there are some important differences between them. European knights were always from a high class in society but *wuxia* heroes can be from a high or a low class. The Japanese *samurai* (Japanese knights) and European knights worked for a master but the typical *wuxia* hero does not. He is more like the western character Robin Hood, a fighter who wants to help people and do good, but also a person who does not always respect the law.

Although a few *wuxia* stories take place in modern times or even in the future, most take place in the *Jianghu* (meaning 'rivers and lakes') of imperial ancient China. *Jianghu* does not refer to a real place – it is like another world inside the real world. It is a world where martial artists and monks, beautiful princesses, thieves and artists live. It is a place where the law and order system does not work well and the only way that people can keep themselves safe is by showing how strong they are. The hero helps them to do this.

Perhaps the most famous writer of *wuxia* fiction in China today is Louis Cha. He is better known to his Chinese fans by his pen name Jin Yong (the name he uses for writing). Many of his stories have been made into films for the cinema and television. In his very popular novels,

> Louis Cha (born 1924) began his career as a journalist in Shanghai and later went to Hong Kong to manage a newspaper. He is so famous that an asteroid (a large piece of rock in space) was given his name in 1998.

the martial artists who live in the *Jianghu* are called the *wulin*. They have a chosen leader called the *Wulin Mengzhu* who is responsible for making sure[P] that there is law and order in *Jianghu*.

Martial arts today

In China the word used for all the martial arts that people in the West call 'kung fu' is *wushu*. *Wu* means military – to do with fighting – and *shu* means skill, so *wushu* means the skill of fighting. Since 1990, the word *wushu* has been used for a style of martial art that is now an international sport. It is not yet an Olympic™ sport like taekwondo and judo, but many people, including the martial arts actor Jackie Chan, think that it should be.

5 Traditional Chinese Medicine

Chinese herbal medicines

Traditional Chinese medicine (TCM) began nearly five thousand years ago in the time of three legendary emperors who lived between 2800 BC and 2600 BC – Fu Xi, Shennong and Huangdi, the Yellow Emperor. Legend says that they taught people all the skills they needed to know to live on earth. The most ancient of them, Fu Xi, taught people how to catch fish, make silk and write. Shennong is called the 'Father of Agriculture[58]' because he taught people to farm. He also taught them about herbal medicine (medicine made from plants) and acupuncture (treating[59] diseases by putting special needles – long, thin pieces of metal – into parts of the body). Huangdi, the Yellow Emperor, is perhaps the most well known of the three. Legend says that his conversations with Qi Bo, a doctor who worked at the Emperor's court, were the basis of[P] China's first medical book, *The Yellow Emperor's Classic of Internal Medicine*. It was probably written in the second century BC, but even today, students of Chinese medicine still read it.

In about 100 BC, during the Han dynasty, China was an important centre for medical studies and the home of some of the world's best doctors. Students studied with them and learnt from them before taking their exams to become doctors themselves. During this period another important medical book was written, *Shennong's Classic of Herbal Medicine*. This book has a list of 365 Chinese medicines, 252 from plants, sixty-seven from animals and forty-six from minerals. More medicines were added in later years: in AD 659 there were 850 on the list.

Many of the ideas doctors had about the causes of diseases and how to treat them were influenced by two Daoist beliefs.

- *yin* and *yang*: opposite forces which depend on each other for their existence. For example, night and day, wet and dry, male and female, etc. *Yin* and *yang* are in everything.
- *qi* (pronounced 'chee'): the energy or life force that moves around the body. Chinese traditional doctors believe that people become ill when the *qi* does not move well. They use exercise, meditation, a good diet and techniques like acupuncture to make it move better.

The yin yang symbol shows the way Daoists understand opposites.

There were many developments in the scientific study of medicines between the third and the tenth centuries. Chinese doctors learnt a lot from doctors in the Middle East and countries like India and Japan, and many important books were written about the causes of diseases and how to treat them. The work of alchemists (people who tried to turn metals into gold, especially during the Middle Ages) was also very important to the development of medicines. Alchemists were the first people to do experiments with different chemicals and minerals and prepare medicines with them. In China many of the Emperors were more interested in living forever[60] than in gold. So, Chinese alchemists tried to create a magic liquid (called the *elixir of life*) that could make it possible to live forever. Ge Hong (283–343), a famous alchemist and doctor at that time, spent all his life looking for the right ingredients. In the end he decided that traditional medicines made from plants could make people healthy and help them live longer, but only medicines made with chemicals and minerals could make people live forever.

In 1330, a court doctor called Hu Sihui wrote a book called *Important Principles of Food and Drink*. In it he suggested that people often become ill because they do not eat correctly. He said they should not eat too much and should eat a balanced[61] diet – the right amount of different types of food. He also included some regional recipes in the book that later became Chinese national dishes.

Li Shizhen (1518–1593), a herbalist[62] and acupuncturist, wrote a book that contained details of more than 1,800 medicines and detailed descriptions of over one thousand plants. It is still an important reference book for herbalists today.

Western medicine was first brought to China in the sixteenth and seventeenth centuries by Christian missionaries[63] but the Chinese continued to prefer their traditional medicines. By the nineteenth century there were many Europeans in China and several modern hospitals. Western medical books were translated into Chinese and doctors started to become more interested in the new types of medicine in the West. Some of them even went to study at western universities. When they returned to China they taught others what they had learnt, so more and more people were introduced to western medicine.

After the end of the Qing dynasty in 1911, traditional Chinese medicine was seen as old-fashioned and some people wanted to stop the practice of it completely. Today, however, it is popular once again and is used side by side[P] with western medicine in many of China's hospitals.

Herbal medicine

The Chinese have known for thousands of years that plants are good for treating diseases. Today many people in the West, too, prefer herbal products to medical drugs, especially to treat less serious problems. They can be bought from health food stores and some pharmacies and, of course, from websites on the Internet. When Chinese people want herbal medicine, they go to see a herbal doctor. He listens to their voice, looks at their eyes, smells their body and feels their pulse[64] in order to understand the problem. Then he gives them a list of ingredients for a medicine (sometimes as many as thirty!). They take the list to a special shop and the person in the shop puts together the correct amounts of the ingredients. The medicines are then used to make teas, soups or creams.

Ginseng has been used by the Chinese for over five thousand years and has been called the 'elixir of life'.

The Shiitake mushroom can help the body fight colds and flu.

The Chinese cucumber is good for a cough.

Acupuncture

Acupuncture is one of the oldest medical techniques in China and is often used to treat pain. According to Daoist philosophy, good health depends on the free movement of *qi* along the meridians (invisible lines or channels in the body). When *qi* cannot move, or is moving too slowly, the result is illness or pain. By putting thin metal needles into certain points along the meridians, the acupuncturist can start the *qi* moving again.

Many famous Hollywood film stars have had acupuncture treatment for many illnesses and problems, including stress.

- Nine different types of acupuncture needles are mentioned in *The Yellow Emperor's Classic of Internal Medicine*.
- The oldest acupuncture needles that have been found go back to AD 600.
- There are about 360 important acupuncture points along the fourteen main meridian lines.

'People bring me their pets when modern medicine hasn't worked for them. Although the animals can't talk, the results after acupuncture are clear and their owners can see the difference for themselves.'

DOCTOR LI – A VET

Qigong

Qigong is any form of martial art that includes breathing techniques, movement and meditation. T'ai chi is a type of qigong. Doing qigong is said to increase and balance *qi* and is especially useful for people who have problems of stress. In China, millions of people, especially older people, do t'ai chi together early in the morning in the parks. They do it not only to keep fit but also to increase their energy levels so they can stay active all day.

World T'ai Chi and Qigong Day is celebrated on the last Saturday of April each year. Tens of thousands of people in over seventy countries take part in organized events.

6 Eating and Drinking in China

A typical Chinese noodle dish

Eating together as a family is an important part of daily life for Chinese people. Families like to sit down together for a meal at least twice a day. In China the food can be more or less the same for every meal, not like in the UK, for example, where people have different food at different times of the day – cereals and milk in the morning for breakfast, a sandwich for lunch, meat and vegetables in the evening for dinner. Chinese breakfasts are usually cooked and hot but the food people eat depends on which part of the country they live in: rice is more common in the south and noodles (long pasta) or bread in the north. For lunch there are always several vegetable and meat or fish dishes. These dishes are eaten with a bowl of rice or noodles. The Chinese do not usually drink cold drinks with meals but they have a light soup or tea. There are many different kinds of dessert, but desserts are not eaten with every meal and are usually not very sweet. Cakes and sweet things are eaten at special events or with small meals at teahouses.

Teahouses

The Chinese have a long history of tea-drinking, and teahouses are very popular places for people to meet friends and relax. Tea is served in a special way and serving tea can be a way of showing respect, welcoming guests or saying sorry. Some people, especially older people, enjoy playing cards or *mahjong* (a Chinese board game) while they drink their tea. Very often, small snacks called *dim sum* are eaten with a cup of tea. This is very popular, especially in southern China.

Dim sum are small Chinese snacks.

Unfortunately, traditional teahouses are disappearing fast because many young people prefer the western-style cafés that are opening all over China.

> 66 *Better to be without food for three days, than without tea for one.* 99
>
> **Ancient Chinese proverb**

Banquets

When Chinese people want to entertain guests, celebrate birthdays, do business and so on, they do not usually invite people to their house to eat. Instead, they have a banquet (a large meal in a restaurant). Most visitors to China are invited to one sooner or later.

Banquets are held in big restaurants. For special events, banquets take place in private rooms. The host[65] and the guests sit at a round table and take food from dishes that are put in the middle of it or on a 'lazy Susan' (a big dish that turns around). It is not considered impolite to reach across someone or pass dishes and it is normal for the host to serve the guests, giving them the best pieces of meat and fish. Sometimes, cold cooked dishes are brought first – vegetables, meat, eggs and fish. Then the hot dishes arrive. These dishes can be traditional Chinese dishes with rice and noodles or western-style ones like steak. There is usually at least one soup and sometimes different types of tea are drunk between the different parts of the meal. There are many, many dishes and always much more food than people can eat.

Balance and harmony

Eating healthy food is very important. According to Chinese cooking philosophy, a meal should be a good balance between the main food – usually rice or noodles (*fan*), and the side dishes – vegetables, fish or meat (*cai*). This is different from a western meal, which often has meat or fish as the main part of the meal. A typical Chinese meal has one *fan* dish, three or four *cai* dishes and a soup. The *cai* dishes are balanced so there is, if possible, one meat, one fish and one vegetable.

A healthy meal must also have the right balance of *yin* and *yang*. *Yin* foods have a lot of water in them and make the body cold; *yang* foods are energy[66] foods and make the body warm. There are some examples in the table on the right.

Yin foods	Yang foods
apples	beef
bananas	carrots
fish	cheese
mushrooms	eggs
pasta	garlic
strawberries	onions
sugar	potatoes
tomatoes	salt

As well as a good balance of *yin* and *yang*, a meal should also contain each of the five main food flavours[67] according to the Chinese. These flavours are sweet, sour, bitter, spicy and salty.

Confucius said that food must be prepared and eaten with harmony, so a good Chinese cook tries to make sure that the colour, shape, smell and taste of a meal all go well together and look good on the table.

Chinese people like having meals together with their relatives and friends because sharing food brings people closer together. Restaurants in China are often very noisy but this shows that people are having a good time and that there is harmony around the table.

Chinese restaurants are also extremely popular in the West today, but the food they serve is sometimes very different from Chinese food in China.

- The first Chinese restaurant in the USA opened in San Francisco in about 1849 when thousands of Chinese people from Canton (Guangdong) went to San Francisco to look for gold.
- In 1907, the first Chinese restaurant in England opened. It was in London and was called *Maxim's*. The food was Cantonese.

The eight regional cuisines[68]

The history of Chinese cuisine is centuries old. Throughout history, techniques and ingredients from the cuisines of other cultures were also adopted as the empire got bigger.

> *South is sweet, North is salty, East is spicy, West is sour.*
>
> **Chinese saying**

Each region in China has its own food culture and the food is a mirror of the region's history, its people and its geography. There are only small differences between some of them but each one has its own flavours and style. Out of the twenty-two provinces, eight have a cuisine that is well known both in China and around the world.

The four most important cuisines are the ones of Shandong, Jiangsu, Guangdong and Sichuan.

Province	Cuisine	Flavour
Shandong	Lu	sweet and sour
Jiangsu	Su	a little sweet
Anhui	Hui	salty
Zhejiang	Zhe	a little salty
Fujian	Min	light, sweet, a little spicy
Guangdong	Yue	bitter
Hunan	Xiang	spicy
Sichuan	Chuan	hot and spicy

Lu is the cuisine of the capital, Beijing. It has a history that goes back to the time of Confucius, who came from a city near Qufu, in Shandong Province.

Seafood (fish, etc.) is an important ingredient in this cuisine. The onion is another. Sweet and sour carp (a fish from the Yellow River) and meat cooked with onions are typical dishes. Because Shandong is in Northern China, people usually eat bread with their meals and not rice.

Su cuisine is light and fresh and includes lots of lake and river fish, seafood, duck and vegetables. The good climate means that farmers can grow many types of vegetables so there is always a lot of choice at the local markets. Su cuisine is famous for its beautiful appearance because Su cooks believe that all dishes should not only taste good but look good too.

Yue cuisine is also known as Cantonese cuisine and is perhaps the most well-known Chinese cooking style outside China. That is because most of the Chinese people who opened restaurants in other countries were from Guangdong province.

Sichuan is famous for its very hot and spicy **chuan** cuisine. Sichuan cooks use a lot of garlic, ginger and chilli pepper in their dishes, most of which are made with meat. The chilli pepper is not a local vegetable – it was introduced into China from South America at the end of the seventeenth century but soon became very popular. A typical dish is Kung Pao chicken. It is made with chicken, peanuts[69], vegetables and chilli peppers.

What to do when eating in China

- Take a present if you are invited to eat in someone's home.
- Use two hands to offer a plate or dish to someone who is older than you.
- Arrive on time for banquets.
- Put your chopsticks across your bowl when you have finished eating.
- Make a noise when you eat noodles or drink soup – it shows that you are enjoying the food.
- Leave some food on your plate at the end of the meal. If you eat everything, your host might think that there was not enough food on the table.

What not to do when eating in China

- Start eating before your host at banquets.
- Put your fingers in your mouth while eating.
- Put salt on your food.
- Play with chopsticks during a meal and point at things with them.

Chopsticks

People began to use chopsticks in the Shang dynasty (1766–1122 BC) when small sticks were probably used for stirring food in pots during cooking. Later, people began cutting food into small pieces because it cooked more quickly. Small pieces of hot food could be eaten without knives and so people used the sticks to eat them. But perhaps Confucius also had something to do with[P] why the Chinese use chopsticks! Confucius believed in peace between people and he said that good people did not allow knives on their table.

Chopsticks are usually made of bamboo and used only once. This is very bad for the environment because many trees are cut down to make them, so some people have now started to use metal or plastic ones.

Chopsticks

- The Chinese word for chopsticks – *kuaizi* – means 'quick little men'. **i**
- In China over forty-five billion pairs of chopsticks are used every year.
- Chinese chopsticks are longer than Japanese or Korean ones.
- There is a chopstick museum in Shanghai.

Tea

❝ *Not for all the tea in China!* **❞**

An old saying in English that means 'nothing you offer me will make me do something'.

Chinese people have been drinking tea for more than five thousand years. At first they drank it as a medicine but now it is part of their daily lives. It is usually drunk without milk or sugar, although in the north-western, Muslim areas people add sugar, and the Tibetans drink their tea with butter!

Tea is grown in the warmer, wetter regions of China, especially in the provinces of Fujian, Yunnan, Anhui and Zhejiang. The most common types – green, black and *oolong* – all have different tastes because the flavour of tea depends on where it comes from.

The province of Zhejiang, for example, is famous all over the world for its Longjing tea, a green tea. The leaves are long and thin and the tea is a yellow-green colour. People like it for its fresh taste and sweet smell. The Qing emperor Kangxi (1654–1722) liked it so much he called it Imperial tea.

- More than eighty million people work in the tea industry in China. **i**
- There are more than eight hundred different Chinese teas.
- The Chinese describe tea according to colour: green tea, blue tea, red tea, white tea, yellow tea and dark green tea.
- The first tea to arrive in Britain came from China in 1652.

Young women picking tea in China

7 Festivals

A lion dancer

There are many different festivals in China – almost as many as the different ethnic groups. There are the big national festivals like Chinese New Year, and also many regional ones. For example, the Uyghur people in Xinjiang, the capital of the Uyghur Autonomous Region, celebrate the Muslim festival of Ramadan; the Dai people in the south-western province of Yunnan celebrate *Po Shui Jie*, or Water Throwing Festival; and the Mongols have a seven-day festival in July or August with martial arts competitions and ball games.

Traditional Chinese Festivals follow the lunar (moon) calendar. This means the dates of some festivals change each year. New Year, National Day and Labour Day are fixed to the western calendar. In Hong Kong, Christmas Day is also a public holiday.

> The Chinese calendar is divided into twelve lunar months of twenty-nine or thirty days. The lunar months begin at the new moon. A year of twelve lunar months is 354 days long. An extra month is added every three or four years so that the seasons are always the same. The first year on the Chinese calendar is the year when China's first legendary Emperor began to rule – 2698 BC. So, 2014 on the western calendar, for example, is 4712 on the Chinese lunar calendar.

Spring Festival (*Chun Jie*) – Chinese New Year

This is the most important Chinese festival and celebrates the end of winter and the beginning of spring. The exact day depends on the date of the new moon, but it is always between 21st January and 19th February. The festival lasts fifteen days and tens of millions of Chinese people travel to their home towns to be with their families. It is the largest yearly movement of people on earth, so many people start their journeys weeks before the holiday in order to find a seat on a train or a plane.

In the days before New Year, people clean their homes. *Duilian* – long pieces of red paper with short poems in beautiful calligraphy on them – are put on both sides of the door and everyone buys new clothes. On the evening before New Year's Day, the family gets together in the evening for a big meal. *Jiaozi* (dumplings[70]), noodles, chicken and fish are all traditional New Year foods. After dinner, *hongbao*, red envelopes containing money, are given to children. At midnight the bells ring and the celebrations start with fireworks[71].

For the next three or more days, families visit their friends and neighbours to wish them a Happy New Year. They take sweets, cakes and fruit like oranges.

> There are seven public holidays in China:
>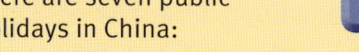
> - 1st January – New Year
> - January/February – Spring Festival/Chinese New Year
> - April – Qingming Festival
> - 1st May – Labour Day
> - May/June – Dragon Boat Festival
> - September – Mid-Autumn Festival
> - 1st October – National Day

A traditional lion dance, which is thought to bring good luck, is often performed at New Year. Two dancers – one for the lion's head and the other for the body – dance through the streets to loud music.

- Birthdays in China are connected with New Year.
- Traditionally, Chinese people become one year older on the seventh day of the New Year, but now many people celebrate western-style birthdays too.
- Some people in China do not celebrate their birthday until they are sixty.
- The Chinese believe that babies are one year old when they are born.
- The first big birthday celebration in a child's life is when he or she is one month old. It is called *Mun-Yut* or the 'red egg and ginger' party.
- On birthdays, Chinese people will eat very long noodles, being careful not to bite and break them. This means that they will have a long life.

Lantern Festival

New Year celebrations end with 'The Festival of Lanterns' on the fifteenth day after the new moon and the first night with a full moon in the Chinese lunar calendar. This is a much quieter event than New Year.

The Lantern Festival in Shanghai

The Lantern Festival has a very long history and there are many stories about how the festival began. Legend says that during the Han dynasty (206 BC–AD 220) when Buddhism became more popular in China, one of the emperors gave an order to light[72] lanterns in the imperial palace on the fifteenth day of the first lunar month to show respect for Buddha. Since then, lighting lanterns has become a tradition for Chinese people. At the time of the festival, red lanterns can be seen in the streets and in every house and shop. Exhibitions of lanterns of many different shapes and sizes in the parks attract many tourists as well as local people.

On the night of the festival, families get together to look at the full moon and eat small dumplings made of rice; *yuanxiou* in northern China, and *tangyuan* in southern China. The round dumplings in a bowl mean harmony and happiness.

Qingming Festival

This April festival is both sad and happy. It is a time when all Chinese people remember the dead. They go and clean the tombs of their relatives and leave food, flowers and other presents for them. But it is springtime and the weather is warmer so it is also a good time to make short trips to the countryside or to the parks to enjoy the fresh air, flowers and trees.

The Dragon Boat Festival (*Duanwu* Festival or Double Fifth)

This festival is on the fifth day of the fifth lunar month, which means it can be in May or June. The main event of the festival is the boat races. The boats are from one to three metres long and there are sometimes as many as eighty people in the longer boats! They are brightly painted for the festival and have a dragon head at the front and a dragon tail at the back. The races are always very exciting and many people go to watch them. Dragon boat racing is popular all over the world and many countries hold their own Dragon Boat Festivals.

> **i**
> - In China dragons are symbols of importance, power and strength.
> - The dragon was also a symbol of the emperor.
> - Chinese emperors wore clothes decorated with dragons.
> - There are nine types of dragon in Chinese culture. Many places in China are called 'Nine Dragons'.

A dragon-boat race

The Mid-Autumn Festival (*Zhong Qiu*)

This festival is on the fifteenth day of the eighth lunar month, between September and October. It is an important holiday and people usually travel home to be with their family. On the night of the fifteenth, everyone goes outside to admire the full moon and eat mooncakes – the typical cakes of this festival.

A legend links the tradition of eating mooncakes during the Mid-Autumn Festival to the Yuan dynasty (1280–1368). It says the Han were not happy with their Mongol rulers, so a group of them planned a rebellion. They wanted other Han to join them but they had to do it in secret. Someone had the idea of hiding a message in the cakes and selling them to the Han. As a result, thousands of people arrived on the night of the rebellion. From then on, people started to eat mooncakes every Mid-Autumn Festival to remember it.

'Some shops sell ice cream mooncakes now. They are really good! My favourite flavour is chocolate.'
JIN – A SCHOOLBOY

The Chinese have celebrated harvest-time during the autumn full moon for more than three thousand years, but the name 'mid-autumn' first appeared in a book written during the Western Zhou Dynasty (1046–771 BC). It described how the emperors and important officials at the court used to go outside to admire the full moon. They used to take a large table outside to the garden and put fruit and other food on it for Chang'e, the moon goddess. However, it was only during the early Tang dynasty (618–907) that the day was officially celebrated as a traditional festival.

Water Throwing Festival

The Water Throwing Festival of the Dai ethnic minority in southern China takes place during their New Year celebrations. It lasts three days. On the last day everybody puts on their best clothes and takes clean water to the Buddhist Temple. They wash the Buddha and then throw the water at each other for luck, happiness and health.

The Water Throwing Festival of the Dai people

The Festival for Lovers (Double Seventh Festival)

This festival is sometimes called China's 'Valentine's Day'. It is on the seventh day of the seventh month of the lunar calendar. As with other traditional Chinese festivals, there is a legend to explain the festival.

In mid-summer it is possible to see the Milky Way (a big group of stars) very clearly in the night sky. Two stars can be more easily seen than the others. The legend says that these are a poor cowherd (a boy who looks after cows) and a weaver maid (a girl who makes cloth for clothes).

They met on earth, fell in love and got married. They were so happy together that the cowherd forgot to look after his cows and the weaver maid forgot to make cloth. The girl's mother, a Queen in Heaven[73], saw this and it made her angry, so she ordered her daughter to return to Heaven. The cowherd tried to follow her but the Queen made the Milky Way so that they could not reach each other. The birds in the sky were sorry for[P] them and, on the seventh day of the seventh month, they made a bridge across the Milky Way for the lovers. Since then, that day has been known as the Festival for Lovers or Double Seventh festival.

- The numbers six, eight, and nine are lucky numbers because their names in Chinese sound like words that have positive meanings.
- The number seven is a lucky number for relationships.
- Four is an unlucky number because it sounds like the word for 'death'. Some hotels in China do not have a fourth floor.

8 Entertainment

Peking opera performers

The Chinese have more than 115 days of holiday a year, including weekends and national holidays. During their free time people like to eat out with their friends, go to clubs to dance, do sports and go shopping. There are also many kinds of entertainment, both traditional and modern, for them to enjoy.

Traditional music

Some of the ethnic minorities, especially the Uyghur, are famous for their music. They play many different types of instruments. These include the *pipa,* a type of guitar with four strings[74] which has been played for almost

two thousand years in China. The *erhu*, a type of violin with two strings, is also very old. As well as performing their music in concert halls, musicians also play in some teahouses.

The traditional Chinese musical forms that are popular today started to develop during the Tang dynasty and music became an important part of Confucian education. Confucius was able to play musical instruments and we think that he also taught music.

> " To educate somebody, you should start with poems, show the importance of ceremonies[75], and finish with music. "
>
> **Confucius**

Western classical music

As well as traditional Chinese music, people also enjoy western classical music. This kind of music was introduced into China at the end of the nineteenth century and now some of the best western classical musicians in the world are Chinese. The young Chinese pianist Lang Lang, for example, is famous around the world and his performances are popular with people of all ages.

China is one of the biggest makers of musical instruments in the world, especially pianos, violins and guitars. In 2011 the country made 351,000 pianos.

Chinese classical pianist, Lang Lang

Traditional theatre

Since the eighteenth century, Peking Opera (*jingxi* or *jingju*) has been the main form of Chinese theatre. Now it is famous all over the world and a visit to a performance is a must[P] for visitors to Beijing.

Jingxi first became popular in the Qing dynasty (1644–1911). It is said that when Emperor Qianlong was visiting the south of the country, he admired the local operas of Anhui and Hubei provinces so much that he took the performers back to Beijing with him. After that the new form of opera developed.

Peking Opera is different from western opera because it includes acrobatics[76] and martial arts as well as music, drama, literature and singing. There is no large orchestra but there is a group of six or seven musicians, who sit on the stage[77] near the performers.

The stories of the operas are often popular legends or historical events. The characters in them can be divided into four groups: the *sheng* (male); and the *dan* (female); the *jing* (characters with painted faces); and the *chou* (comic characters). The *sheng* and the *dan* have natural faces, not painted ones. In the past, only men were allowed to be in the operas, but since 1912 both men and women can take part. However, a few men have become very famous for playing *dan* parts.

The clothes of the performers are important because they help people understand who is the hero, the bad man, the fighter and so on.

> One of the favourite *jing* characters is the Monkey King, who is the hero of the Chinese traditional story called *Journey to the West*. It was written in the sixteenth century, probably by Wu Cheng'en, a poet and writer, and is one of the greatest books of Chinese literature. It is an exciting adventure story which is based on many Buddhist and Daoist beliefs. A film by the Chinese director/producer, Stephen Chow, based on the book appeared in the cinema in 2013.

The make-up and the colours of the painted faces of the *jing* also help: red, blue and black are for good people; white is for a bad person; purple is for a serious person; and green is for an angry person.

These days, the operas that have lots of martial arts and acrobatics are the most popular, especially with young people and visitors from other countries. In the romantic operas the skill of the singers is more important and the acrobatics are used in the dances.

The Peking Opera has appeared in many Chinese films. One of the most well known in the West is *Farewell My Concubine* (1993), by the Chinese director Chen Kaige.

The circus[78]

Another form of traditional entertainment is the circus. Although there are some acts with animals, most of them are acrobatic. In one of the most popular acrobatic acts, twenty or more people all stand on a bicycle. Other circus acts include men who eat fire and Shaolin monks who do kung fu kicks and jumps.

There are still many travelling circuses that go from town to town in the countryside, but the most famous circus in China is probably the Chinese State Circus. Like the Peking Opera, it is also very popular with tourists. The shows are based on acrobatic acts, which are introduced by the Monkey King. There are singers and dancers from the Peking Opera, a lion dance and sometimes acrobatics in the air. The Chinese State Circus was started by Phillip Gandey, an Englishman, in the 1990s. It is based in Beijing but spends much of the year travelling in other countries.

Shadow puppet plays

Shadow puppet plays are an ancient way of telling stories for entertainment and there are still puppet theatres all over China today.

The puppet characters are made of thick paper or leather[79] and they are moved by a person behind a white screen so that the audience see the shadow of the puppet. As well as the person moving the puppets, there are also three musicians and a

Chinese shadow puppets

55

person who sings the story. There are many kinds of stories: historical ones which last hours and hours, love stories and ghost stories, stories about wars and battles and comedies.

Puppet theatres and puppet shows are very popular with both children and adults. There is a regular National Puppet Show and Shadow Play Competition in the city of Xi'an and prizes are given to the best puppets and the best stories.

Board games

China is well known for its board games. *Go*, the oldest board game in the world, started in China more than 2,500 years ago, and people around the world still enjoy playing it today! Another Chinese game, *Mahjong,* was first played in the 1800s. Today the city of Chengdu is famous for this game – almost everyone there knows how to play it. They play it on the

- *Mahjong* probably started as a card game called *Ma-Tiao*.
- The game is played by four people.
- It is played with 136 or 144 tiles (pieces).
- Players must match pictures or Chinese characters on the tiles to win.

streets, in teahouses, in *mahjong* houses or at their homes. Chengdu people believe that playing *mahjong* is useful and good for their health.

Playing games has always been a popular way of passing the time with older people but now many younger people find it a good way to relax after spending the day on the computer. In Beijing there are more than two hundred board game cafés – small places with comfortable chairs and lines of tables where groups of friends can choose a game from the hundreds on the shelves to play.

Flying kites

This is another traditional activity enjoyed by people, young and old, especially during the Qingming Festival in April, when it is windy. The parks, gardens and city squares are crowded with people flying kites of all colours and shapes. Sometimes they put little coloured lanterns on the tails of their kites and fly them in the evening when it is dark. Then the lanterns look like stars in the night sky. In the past, people cut the string to let the kite fly freely. This custom is believed to bring good luck and keep away diseases.

Flying kites is a traditional hobby in China.

Modern music

In the bigger cities there are many clubs where young people can listen to live music. There are also several big music festivals every year for music fans. For example, the Midi Modern Music Festival in Beijing takes place during the May holiday. This is a big music concert that attracts hundreds of musicians, who perform every kind of modern music from rock and metal to punk and jazz.

Karaoke

An extremely popular form of entertainment is KTV – China's name for karaoke. People go to a special place, usually a club, where they can sing and have fun with friends. Young people like celebrating birthdays at a KTV

57

club, and businessmen go there to relax after work. The songs are in both English and Chinese.

KTV clubs usually have a big room where visitors can share the karaoke machine with other guests. During big holidays these rooms are crowded and everyone celebrates together. If people are having a special party, they can also pay for a private room. Karaoke is so popular that some clubs are open twenty-four hours a day.

'I have enjoyed every single moment in China so far. My first experience at a KTV club was great and is one of the best memories. I would like to go back there again while I am in Beijing.'
ARISA – AN AMERICAN WORKING IN BEIJING

Cinema

The number of people who go to the cinema has grown a lot recently in China. Today, there are almost as many as in the USA, which is the country that has the highest number at the moment. By 2020 there will be more than in the USA! Because of this, China is building thousands of new cinemas.

At the moment, not many foreign films are shown in China but the number is growing because they are so popular. In 2011, for example, in the list of the top ten films that made the most money in China only four were Chinese. The others were American. Although there are fewer of them, foreign films usually make much more money than Chinese ones. However, in December 2012 the comedy *Lost in Thailand* made Chinese film history by becoming the first Chinese film to make over one billion yuan.

Since the 1980s, some Chinese film directors have become well known outside China because their films have won prizes at international film festivals. Zhang Yimou and Chen Kaige are probably the most famous. Their prize-winning films include:

There were fewer than 1,300 cinemas in China in 2002. At the end of 2012 there were more than 13,000.

- *Red Sorghum* by Zhang Yimou (winner Berlin Film Festival 1988)
- *Farewell my Concubine* by Chen Kaige (winner Cannes Film Festival 1993)
- *Together* by Chen Kaige (best director San Sebastian Film Festival 2002)

Going to the cinema in China can be an expensive experience as tickets cost quite a lot. It can also be a noisy experience! People like to eat and talk while they are watching a film, and they do not usually switch off their mobile phones. Europeans and Americans find this distracting[80] but the Chinese do not seem to mind at all!

Jackie Chan is a very famous actor who has worked both in China and Hollywood. He is known for his acrobatic fighting style. He has been acting since the 1960s and has made over 150 films.

9 China in the Twentieth Century

Deng Xiaoping

Chinese people have not always been able to enjoy doing the activities they can do now, like watching Hollywood films or travelling. The twentieth century was a very difficult time for China – it was a period of great change and life was not easy for many people. But by the end of the century, China had become a modern nation with a growing economy.

The century began under the rule of the Manchu Qing dynasty. China was weak because the Manchus had not governed the country well for many years. They were very unpopular with the Han, who wanted them to leave the country. In 1911 there was a revolution and China became a republic governed by the Chinese Nationalist Party. After a short civil war between the Nationalists and the Communists, the Communists took control in 1949 and the People's Republic of China was founded.

Four men played a large part in the important changes in China in the twentieth century – Sun Yat-sen, Chiang Kai-shek, Mao Zedong and Deng Xiaoping.

1644–1911	1911–1949	1949–2000	i
Qing dynasty	Republic of China under the Nationalists	The People's Republic of China under the Communists	

Sun Yat-sen (1866–1925) – The Father of the Country

Sun Yat-sen's father was a peasant[81] farmer. Sun was born in China but he moved to Hawaii as a child to live with his older brother. Sun's brother paid for Sun to have a good education. Sun went to an English-speaking school in Honolulu, Hawaii, and later studied medicine in Hong Kong.

But Sun did not become a doctor. While he was studying, he became a revolutionary. He helped organize several revolutions against the Manchus but all of them failed. Finally, in 1911, the Manchu dynasty was defeated. Sun was in America when this happened, but when he heard, he quickly returned to China. There he became President of a united China.

Sun Yat-sen wanted China to be a modern nation and use western methods in industry and farming. He believed that China had to become a Republic because it needed to be as strong as the West.

Sun Yat-sen

But there was another revolution in 1913. An army officer called Yuan Shikai took control and Sun had to escape to Japan.

He returned home in 1917 after Yuan died and in the following years he re-organized the Nationalist party and made it stronger. The Communists, who had formed a political party in 1921, joined them because both parties wanted the same thing – a united China.

The Nationalists needed an army, so Sun started a military academy in Guangzhou where soldiers could learn to be officers. He made his friend Chiang Kai-shek the director of the academy.

When Sun died in 1925, China was still not united. In later years, the Nationalists and the Communists became enemies and there was a civil war for many years, which ended in 1949.

> **i** Aisin Gioro, or Pu Yi, became the last Qing emperor in 1908, at the age of three. After the Nationalists took control, he continued to live in the Forbidden City until 1924. The Communists put him in prison in 1950 but he was allowed to go free in 1959. He died in 1967 after working for seven years as a gardener in Beijing.

Chiang Kai-shek (1887–1975)

Chiang Kai-shek was born in Zhejiang, in eastern China. At the age of eighteen he went to a military college in Japan. He returned to China in 1911 for the rebellion against the Qing Dynasty. Later, he joined the Nationalist party because he admired Sun Yat-sen. After Sun's death in 1925, Chiang became the leader of the party. At first, the Nationalists and the Communists worked together to unite China, but in 1927 the two parties separated and were at war with each other.

In the same year, Chiang married Soong Mei-ling. She was the youngest of three daughters of Charles Soong, the son of poor peasants who had gone to live in Boston, USA. He later returned to Shanghai and became an important and rich businessman. Mei-ling's older sister, Soong Ching-ling, had been married to Sun Yat-sen.

Chiang's power increased and in less than a year the Nationalists controlled the rich provinces of southern, central and eastern China, where many people lived. The Nationalists killed many Communists at this time and many others had to escape to the countryside in the southeast. In 1934 Chiang planned to attack them in their hiding place in Jiangxi Province, but the Communists escaped. Thousands of them, including Mao Zedong and Deng Xiaoping, who later became leaders of the Communist Party, walked more than 9,000 kilometres from Jiangxi Province to Shaanxi Province in the north. Many people died during the journey. Their journey, known as 'The Long March', is famous in modern Chinese history.

> **i** Madame Chiang Kai-shek, Soong Mei-ling, was famous around the world as a beautiful, intelligent and extremely powerful woman. After Chiang's death in 1975, she went to live in New York. She died in 2003 at the age of 105.

In 1931 the Japanese, a strong military power in the East, attacked north-east China (Manchuria) and then started to move south. By 1937 Japan controlled a lot of northern China. Chiang now needed the help of the Communists to help him fight the Japanese. In 1945, when the Second World War ended, Japan was defeated and the Japanese left China. However, in the following year, the civil war between the Nationalists and the Communists started again. It finally ended three years later, in 1949, when the Communist soldiers defeated Chiang's army. Chiang and the Nationalists had to escape to Taiwan.

On 1ˢᵗ October in Beijing, Mao Zedong founded the People's Republic of China.

Mao Zedong

Mao was born on 26ᵗʰ December 1893 into a peasant family in Shaoshan, in Hunan Province, central China. After studying to be a teacher, he travelled to Beijing where he worked in the University Library. In 1921, he helped to found the Chinese Communist Party (CCP), which defeated the Nationalists in 1949.

China was a very weak country after years of bad government and war. Mao and other Communist leaders believed that they could create a new, stronger Chinese society, without social classes, by changing the traditional ways of governing the country. Their dream was a powerful and united China.

Mao wanted to have complete control of the country so there was only one political party – the Communist party. He did not allow any other parties. Between 1949 and the 1970s the rest of the world knew very little about what was happening in China because there was very little international communication.

Statue of Mao Zedong in Shenyang

At first, the Soviet Union (USSR) helped the Chinese Communists but in the 1950s the relationship between the two countries was not very good. Mao decided that China must learn to look after itself and not depend on help from outside.

To do that, China needed to become more modern. It needed to grow more of its own food and make more products in factories.

The main changes made by Mao

- The State owned everything and took control of all the factories
- Land was organized into 'collective farms' – large groups of farms which were owned by the State but controlled by the workers
- Foreign businesses were not allowed
- Private banks were closed and a new bank owned by the government was opened

So in 1957 Mao put into action a five-year plan to make China a stronger country. Families were put together to live in large groups called communes, sharing all the work from cooking to looking after the children. Many people were sent to work in small factories to produce steel[82]. Farmers were told to change their ways of farming.

After three years, it was clear that the plan was not working. There were several reasons for this. One was that too many people were working in factories and not enough on the land. Another reason was that the new farming methods did not work and less food was produced. There were also bad floods and bad harvests during those three years. The result was that many thousands of people died because there wasn't enough to eat. So the country had to go back to more traditional ways of producing food.

From the 1950s to the 1990s, most Chinese people, men and women, wore a suit called a *zhifu*, or Mao suit. It was made of dark blue or grey cotton. They are still worn by some Chinese leaders during important state ceremonies and events.

A Mao suit

In 1966, Mao introduced the 'Cultural Revolution'. He was afraid that old ways and old traditions were returning to China and that a middle class was developing. He told young people – schoolchildren and students – to go out and destroy the 'Four Olds' in the country: Old Customs, Old Culture, Old Habits and Old Ideas. These young people called themselves 'Red Guards'. People in the cities were sent to work on farms so that they could learn about life there. Schools and universities were closed and some teachers were put in prison. Traditional paintings and old books were destroyed, and some people in the Communist party lost their jobs.

In the 1970s, Mao started to build better relationships with the United States, Japan and Europe. In 1972, he invited the President of the USA, Richard Nixon, to visit China. It was the first time that Communist China had received a visit from an important western politician and it was a sign of change.

In 1961, the thoughts of Mao were written in a small book called the 'Little Red Book'. It was given to all the Red Guards.

Deng Xiaoping

Deng took part in the Long March with Mao Zedong and was part of his government. But when Deng tried to introduce some economic reforms[83] in 1976, he lost his job because Mao disagreed.

After Mao died, Deng got his job back. Although he never had the highest position in the CCP – General Secretary – Deng was the power behind the next party leaders. He was able to make the changes that were necessary for China to become a world economy.

One of Deng's first reforms was to end the communes and allow the peasants to work on their own pieces of land. Food production soon increased, and other reforms followed. People in the cities were allowed to start small businesses and everyone was allowed to buy things with their own money. From 1978, China's relationship with the rest of the world started to get better. Students travelled to other countries to study, businessmen did business outside China and learning English suddenly became very popular. Foreign students and tourists began to visit China in large numbers as well.

As part of his economic reform plan, Deng created four Special Economic Zones (SEZ) in 1979. These are areas where foreign companies can do business in China. The fishing village of Shenzhen on the border

with Hong Kong was one of them. In 1984, thirty thousand people lived there. In 2011 there were more than ten million.

In 1980, Deng met the British Prime Minister, Margaret Thatcher, to talk about Hong Kong. Three years later the United Kingdom agreed to give Hong Kong back to China in 1997. In 1987, Portugal agreed to give back Macau by 1999.

Deng did not live long enough to see the return of Hong Kong or Macau. He died in February 1997 at the age of ninety-two.

> *It is not important if a cat is black or white. If it catches mice it is a good cat. (Meaning: It is the result of an action that is important, not what is used to do it.)*

Deng Xiaoping

10 China: a Modern Country and a Global Power

Pudong, Shanghai

The new Special Economic Zones created by Deng Xiaoping made it easy for foreign companies to make their products in Chinese factories. They could also build new factories there. The new factories meant that millions of Chinese people could find a job. At the same time China was also making and exporting its own products like toys and clothes, which were much cheaper than the same things made in the West.

Foreign companies not only brought work, they also brought technology. Very quickly, China learnt how to produce high-tech products like televisions, mobile phones, computers, software and modern medicines. Now China is designing and developing these products too.

Deng's economic reforms continued through the 1980s and the 1990s and by 2000 China was on the way to becoming a global power.

2001	China joins the World Trade Organization (WTO).
2002	China plays in the football World Cup.
2003	China sends a man into space for the first time. The astronaut is Yang Liwei.
2004	China hosts several important international events including the first Shanghai Grand Prix.
2004	Zhang Yimou's film 'Hero' makes $49 million in the first month it is shown in the USA.
2005	October – China sends two astronauts into space in the Shenzhou VI capsule.
2006	The Three Gorges Dam, the world's largest water power project, is officially opened.
2008	China hosts the Olympic Games™ and gets 51 gold medals.
2008	September – astronaut Zhai Zhigang completes China's first spacewalk.
2009	China becomes the largest market for cars in the world.
2010	Shanghai hosts the 2010 World Expo (World's Fair – a large public exhibition).
2011	China becomes the world's second largest economy.
2012	More people live in cities than in the countryside in China.

There were 1.11 billion Chinese people with mobile phones at the end of 2012.

The Beijing Olympics™

The 2008 summer Olympics (8th–24th August) and Paralympics (6th–17th September) were very important for China. They told the world that China was once again a country of international importance – that China was now a global superpower[84].

The Games cost $40 billion and took seven years to prepare for. Nineteen new buildings were built especially for the Games. The largest and most important was the National Stadium, where the opening and closing ceremonies were held. The National Stadium cost about $423 million to build and can hold more than ninety thousand people. The

The National Stadium, known as 'The Bird's Nest' because of its appearance

other important new building was the National Aquatics Centre for the water events. It has five swimming pools, a restaurant and seats for seventeen thousand people.

The opening ceremony officially began at eight seconds past eight o'clock on 8th August 2008. That was because the number eight is a lucky number in China and means prosperity. Over fifteen thousand performers took part in the ceremony, which lasted four hours and was full of references to ancient Chinese art and culture.

i

China's performance at the summer Olympic Games™ between 1984 and 2012

Year	Position	Gold medals
1984	4th	15
1988	11th	5
1992	4th	16
1996	4th	16
2000	3rd	28
2004	2nd	32
2008	1st	51
2012	2nd	38

10,942 athletes from 204 countries competed in twenty-eight sports and 302 events. There were many exciting moments and two men in particular made Olympic history. The American swimmer Michael Phelps won eight gold medals and Jamaica's Usain Bolt won the men's 100 metres with a new world record of 9.69 seconds. The Chinese team won the most gold medals of the Games (fifty-one). The gymnast[85] Kai Zou won three of them.

The city of Beijing changed a lot with the Games. It became really modern and international. Old buildings were pulled down and many new roads and modern buildings were built. In 2001, there were 60 kilometres of metro[86] lines, but in 2008 there were 200 kilometres! There are plans to make the lines even longer by 2015. A new terminal[87], T3, was built at the Beijing Capital International Airport to receive all the foreign visitors that wanted to come to see the events. Almost four kilometres long and seven floors high, it is the second largest passenger terminal building in the world.

'The Games produced a greater interest in athletics all around China. Before, there were places, especially smaller cities, where people did not do much sport at all. Now, they do more.'
HONG – A BUSINESSMAN

Perhaps the most important result of the Olympics, however, was that many Chinese people felt proud of their country because China showed the best of itself.

The 2010 World Expo

Two years after the Olympic Games in Beijing, another big international event brought lots of people from all over the world to China. It was the 2010 World Expo in Shanghai. The name of the exhibition was *Better City – Better Life* and was a reference to Shanghai as the 'next great world city' in the twenty-first century.

The 2010 World Expo was the largest and most expensive World Expo ever held. Shanghai spent over $55 billion on preparations for it. New building projects included two new airport terminals, the world's longest metro system, new roads, parks and bridges.

Lang Lang, Jackie Chan and the Italian singer Andrea Bocelli were just some of the performers at the opening ceremony on 30th April 2010.

About seventy-three million people visited the exhibition during the six months that it was open. Most of them were Chinese but 4.25 million of them were foreign visitors.

Shanghai is the largest city in China. It has over twenty-three million people. During the last twenty years, new metal and glass buildings, museums, cultural centres, shopping centres, business and technology parks, universities, restaurants and sports centres have changed the appearance of the city. Pudong, on the Huangpu River's east bank, is Shanghai's newest business area. It has some of the world's tallest office buildings, including the 101-floor World Financial Centre, China's tallest building.

The most popular parts of the city with visitors and tourists, however, are the historical areas in the centre, especially the Bund. The Bund is a road with many beautiful old buildings – including hotels, banks, offices and clubs – from the late nineteenth and early twentieth centuries.

The World Financial Centre

In October 2012, more than three hundred competitors took part in the second Sky Marathon race in the Shanghai World Financial Centre. They ran up one hundred floors, covering 2,754 stairs and 474 metres. The winner climbed to the top in 18 minutes and 55 seconds.

Chinese culture goes global

International events like the Beijing Olympics and the World Expo in Shanghai, and the rise of China as a global power have created a lot of interest in

> *The man who moves a mountain begins by carrying away small stones.*
>
> **Confucius**

Chinese culture and, especially, the Chinese language. Some reports say that more than forty million foreigners around the world are learning Chinese now! Many people think it will soon be as important as English and that it is the language of the future.

More and more parents want their children to learn it. They think it will be a useful skill for their sons and daughters to have. China is the second largest economic power now, so many business people need it because their companies want to do business there.

'If you can speak with Chinese people in their language, you are showing respect for them. It helps to create a good relationship and that is important in business.'
LAURA – A BUSINESSWOMAN

In 2004, the first Confucius Institute opened in Seoul, South Korea. Now there are hundreds of them in cities all over the world. The aim of the Institutes is to help people learn the Chinese language and understand the country and its culture better.

Inside China, The Beijing Language and Culture University receives many young foreign students every year who want to study Chinese. As part of their studies, they also visit famous tourist attractions like the Great Wall and the Peking Opera, and learn the ancient art of t'ai chi and how to cook Chinese food.

Interest in Chinese culture is not a new thing, however. The West has been interested in it since traders began taking first silk, and later, porcelain and tea, to the Roman Empire along the Silk Road. In the nineteenth century, Chinese people took their cuisine to the countries they went to live in, and today there is a lot of interest in martial arts, traditional Chinese medicine and the Chinese film industry.

China: the present and the future

China has developed very quickly since the end of the twentieth century. Its economy is doing well and people have jobs and more money to spend. In the past many people left the country to look for the 'American Dream' in the USA, but now they are moving back to China to follow the 'Chinese Dream'. The same is true for Chinese students who go abroad to finish their studies. Many used to stay in the country where they studied but they prefer to return home now because life is good there and they can find a good job.

However, China is still a country of big differences. Most of the money in China today, for example, belongs to people who are younger than forty-five and living in cities. In the countryside, many people are still very poor and life is hard for them.

So, what is the future for China? Some people think that it could become the next world superpower. It is a big country with a large population. It has a strong economy and a growing global culture. It has military power. It is also a leader in satellite[88] technology and could soon become a leader in space technology. Other people think that superpowers belong to the past, and that in the future the world will be divided into three regional powers: the USA, Europe and the East.

We will have to wait and see[P], but one thing is certain – as a superpower or as a regional power, China will play an important part in the world's future.

China in space

2003 – China became the third country to put a human into space.

2005 – Two astronauts were sent into space.

2008 – Astronaut Zhai Zhigang completed China's first spacewalk.

2012 – China's first female astronaut, Liu Yang, was part of a team sent into space.

2020 – China plans to complete a space station.

Shenzhou space rocket

Points For Understanding

1

1. Why do people in the city of Beijing sometimes find it difficult to see?
2. How did the Yellow River get its name?
3. Which ethnic minority group lives in the Xinjiang Autonomous Region?
4. Why is 1st July 1997 an important date?
5. Who was Pu Yi?
6. Which form of spoken Chinese is the main language of China?

2

1. What was found in Emperor Qin Shi-huang's tomb?
2. Who was Laozi?
3. When did Buddhist temples become centres of learning?
4. During which dynasty was paper money used for the first time?
5. Which Emperor made Beijing his capital city?
6. Why did the Han Chinese think that the Qing were not governing the country well?

3

1. What did Europeans call porcelain?
2. What colour are celadons?
3. What does the word 'calligraphy' mean?
4. What does a calligrapher use to write with?
5. How were literati paintings different from those done by professional painters?
6. What is Song Dong's art work *Waste Not* made of?

4

1 Which emperor introduced fighting systems into China and when?
2 How is the internal style of fighting different from the external style?
3 Why did Bodhidharma start doing physical exercises with the monks?
4 Why did the Qing burn down the Shaolin temples?
5 What does *wuxia* mean?
6 What name does the writer Louis Cha use on his books?

5

1 Why is Shennong called 'the Father of Agriculture'?
2 What is *qi* and why is it important in TCM?
3 What did the doctor Ge Hong spend his life doing and why?
4 Who took Western medicine to China and when?
5 Which plant is called 'the elixir of life'?
6 Why do Chinese people do t'ai chi?

6

1 In which part of China are noodles and bread more common?
2 What are *cai* and *fan*?
3 What are the five main flavours of food in China?
4 Why is Cantonese cuisine very well known outside China?
5 What is Longjing tea like?
6 Why are plastic or metal chopsticks better for the environment than bamboo ones?

7

1 What do Chinese children receive as a present at New Year?
2 How is the Chinese calendar different from the Western one?
3 When are *yuanxiou* dumplings eaten and why are they round?
4 Why did emperors choose the dragon as their symbol?
5 What do Chinese people celebrate during the Mid-Autumn Festival?
6 Why do some hotels in China not have a fourth floor?

8

1 What is a *pipa*?
2 How can people understand who the characters in Peking Opera are?
3 When did the Chinese start playing *mahjong*?
4 Why do many Chinese parents want their children to study music?
5 How do young Chinese people like celebrating birthdays?
6 Why did the film *Lost in Thailand* make history in 2012?

9

1 Why did Sun Yat-sen want China to become a republic?
2 Why did the Communists make 'The Long March' in 1934?
3 Why didn't Mao Zedong's five-year plan work?
4 What were the 'Four Olds' and why did Mao want to destroy them?
5 Why was President Richard Nixon's visit to China in 1972 important?
6 What important reform did Deng Xiaoping make in 1979?

10

1 Why was it important for China to host the Olympic Games™?
2 Why were the Olympic Games™ good for the city of Beijing?
3 How many foreign visitors went to the 2010 World Expo in Shanghai?
4 Why is the Bund especially popular with foreign visitors to Shanghai?
5 Why were Confucius Institutes started?
6 Why is China a country of big differences?

Glossary

1 **government** (page 4)
   the people who control a country, region or town and make decisions
   about its laws and taxes. If you control a country, region or town in this
   way, you *govern* it.

2 **ethnic minority group** (page 6)
   a group of people with the same culture and traditions who live in
   a place where most people have a different culture and different
   traditions

3 **landscape** (page 6)
   an area of land that is beautiful to look at or that has a particular type
   of appearance.

4 **civilization** (page 6)
   a society that has developed its own culture and institutions

5 **emperor** (page 6)
   a number of countries ruled by one person or government is called
   an *empire* and the man who rules an empire is called an *emperor*. A
   woman who rules an empire is called an *empress*. We use the adjective
   imperial to talk about or describe an empire or its rulers.

6 **economy** (page 6)
   the whole of a country's business, industry and trade, and the money
   that they produce

7 **social class** (page 6)
   one of the groups into which people in a society are divided according
   to their family background, education, job or income

8 **revolution** (page 6)
   a situation in which people completely change their government or
   political system, usually by force

9 **symbol** (page 7)
   a picture or shape used to represent something

10 **plateau** (page 8)
   China has many different areas of countryside that have a particular
   type of appearance. There are *plateaus* – large flat areas of land that are
   higher than the land around them – in the south-west. In the south and

east there are areas of land that are low and flat called *lowlands*. Here, there are big rivers with *deltas* – areas where rivers divide into several smaller rivers that *flow*, or move continuously in one direction, into the sea. The rivers have huge *basins* – large areas of land whose surface water all flows into a particular river or lake. In these deltas and basins, the land is *fertile* – able to produce good crops or plants.

11 **humid** (page 8)

humid weather is hot and wet in a way that makes you feel uncomfortable

12 **border** (page 9)

the official line separating two countries or regions

13 **tiger** (page 9)

a large Asian wild animal that has yellowish fur with black lines and is a member of the cat family.

14 **camel** (page 9)

a large animal with a long neck and one or two humps – large round raised parts – on its back. It is often used in deserts for carrying people or things.

15 **trade** (page 9)

the activities of buying and selling goods or services. The *trade routes* were the ways that ships took to carry their goods to other places and bring other goods back again. The trade route called *the Silk Road* was the way that was used to transport *silk* – a smooth cloth made from the fibres produced by an insect called a silkworm.

16 **project** (page 9)

a planned piece of work that has a particular aim, especially one that is organized by a government, company or other organization

17 **inspired** – *to inspire someone* (page 10)

to give someone the idea for a piece of work

18 **birthplace** (page 10)

the place where someone was born or where something first started to exist

19 **sorrow** (page 10)

great sadness

20 **workshop** (page 11)

a room or building where things are made using tools and machines

21 **belief** (page 11)
   an idea that you are certain is true, especially involving religion or
   politics
22 **system** (page 12)
   a method of organizing or doing things
23 **official** (page 14)
   decided by a government
24 **clay** (page 15)
   a type of heavy, wet soil that becomes hard when it is baked in a special
   oven called a kiln, used for making cups, plates and other objects
25 **archeologist** (page 15)
   archeology is the study of ancient societies, done by looking at tools,
   bones, buildings and other things from that time that have been found.
   Someone who studies *archeology* is an *archeologist*.
26 **chariot** (page 15)
   a vehicle with two wheels and no roof that was pulled by horses in
   races and battles in ancient times
27 **prosperity** (page 16)
   the situation of being successful and having a lot of money
28 **printing** (page 16)
   the process of making books, newspapers etc, using a printing press to
   put words and pictures onto paper
29 **increased** – *to increase* (page 16)
   to become larger in amount or number
30 **legendary** (page 16)
   a *legend* is an old story about famous people and events in the past.
   Legends are not usually true. Something that is mentioned or described
   in a legend is described as *legendary*. *Legendary* is also used to describe
   real people who are very famous or well known for a long time.
   Emperor Huangdi is very well known in history.
31 **conquered** – *to conquer something* (page 17)
   to take control of land or people using soldiers
32 **force** (page 17)
   someone or something that has a powerful influence on what happens.
   The *forces of nature* are powerful aspects of nature and the weather, for
   example life and death, and wind and storms.

33 **rebelled** – *to rebel* (page 18)
   to try to remove a government or leader using force. Someone who tries to do this is a *rebel* and the action of doing this is called *rebellion*.
34 **temple** (page 18)
   a building used for worship in some religions, typically religions other than Christianity
35 **founded** – *to found something* (page 18)
   to start an organization, company, political party, etc.
36 **defeated** – *to defeat someone* (page 18)
   to win against someone in a game, fight or election
37 **monk** (page 20)
   a man who lives in a religious community and lives by the rules of a religion
38 **harvest** (page 20)
   the amount of a *crop* – a plant grown for food – that is collected
39 **port** (page 21)
   an area of water where ships stop, including the buildings around it
40 **ink** (page 22)
   a black or coloured liquid used for writing, drawing or printing
41 **civil war** (page 22)
   civil means relating to the people of a country, especially when they are protesting or fighting about something. A *civil war* is a war fought between different groups of people within the same country.
42 **glaze** (page 23)
   a clear, shiny oil that you put on paintings or on objects made of clay, leather or paper to protect them and make them look attractive
43 **decorate** – *to decorate something* (page 23)
   to make something look more attractive by putting nice things on it or in it
44 **last** – *to last* (page 25)
   to continue existing or happening for, or until, a particular time
45 **skill** (page 25)
   a particular ability that involves special training and experience
46 **pottery** (page 26)
   objects such as plates and cups that are made out of clay and baked in an oven so that they become hard

47 **harmony** (page 26)
a situation in which people live and work well with other people, or in a way that does not damage things around them
48 **bamboo** (page 26)
a tall tropical plant with thick, light-brown stems that are used for making things such as furniture and fences
49 **master** (page 27)
a famous artist
50 **performance** (page 27)
the act of *performing* – doing something in front of an audience in order to entertain them, for example in a play, dance or other form of entertainment. Someone who gives a *performance* is a *performer*.
51 **technique** (page 28)
a method of doing something using a special skill that you have developed
52 **improve** – *to improve something* (page 28)
to make something better
53 **mental** (page 28)
relating to the mind
54 **cave** (page 29)
a large hole in the side of a hill or under the ground
55 **meditation** (page 29)
quiet thought that helps you to relax or that is intended as a spiritual or religious exercise
56 **destroyed** – *to destroy something* (page 29)
to damage something so severely that it no longer exists or can never return to its normal state
57 **medieval** (page 31)
relating to the period of European history between about the year 1000 AD and the year 1500. In this period in Europe, there were knights – soldiers from a high social class who wore a metal suit and rode a horse.
58 **agriculture** (page 33)
the work, business or study of farming
59 **treating** – *to treat something* (page 33)
to use medicine or medical methods to cure a patient or an illness. A method for treating illness is called a *treatment*.

60 **forever** (page 34)

for all time in the future, or for as long as you can imagine. If you live *forever*, you do not die.

61 **balanced** (page 35)

with all parts combining well together or existing in the correct amounts

62 **herbalist** (page 35)

someone who grows, sells or prepares *herbs* – plants used as medicine

63 **missionary** (page 35)

someone who has been sent to a place by a religious organization to teach the people there about a particular religion

64 **pulse** (page 35)

the regular movement of blood as the heart pumps it round the body

65 **host** (page 39)

someone who invites people to a meal or party, or to stay in their home

66 **energy** (page 40)

a supply of physical power that you have for doing things that need physical effort. An *energy food* gives you more of this power.

67 **flavour** (page 40)

the particular taste that food or drink has. *Sweet* foods, like *strawberries* – small soft red fruit with a lot of very small seeds on the skin – taste like sugar. *Sour* foods, have a taste like lemons. Something that is *bitter* has a strong sharp taste that is not sweet. For example, *onions* – round vegetables with thin dry skin and many layers inside that taste and smell very strong, and *garlic* – a round white vegetable with small sections called cloves which you add to food for a strong pleasant flavour. *Spicy* food has a strong hot flavour like curry, and *salty* foods contain salt, or taste like salt.

68 **cuisine** (page 41)

a particular style of cooking food, especially the style of a particular country or region

69 **peanut** (page 42)

a type of nut that grows under the ground inside a thin shell and that can be eaten

70 **dumpling** (page 46)
   a small solid lump of cooked food made from flour and water,
   sometimes eaten with meat or added to soup

71 **firework** (page 46)
   an object that explodes when you light it and produces coloured lights
   and loud noises

72 **light** – *to light something* (page 48)
   to make something start to burn, for example, a *lantern* – a light inside
   a transparent container. *Lanterns* are often made of paper and used in
   festivals in China.

73 **heaven** (page 51)
   the place where God or the gods are believed to live

74 **string** (page 52)
   one of several long pieces of nylon, wire or another substance stretched
   across a musical instrument, and used for producing sounds

75 **ceremony** (page 53)
   a formal public event with special traditions, actions or words

76 **acrobatics** (page 54)
   an *acrobat* is someone who can balance, jump and turn their body
   in skilful ways, especially as a form of entertainment. The skills or
   movements of an acrobat are called *acrobatics*.

77 **stage** (page 54)
   the part of a theatre where the actors or musicians perform

78 **circus** (page 55)
   a show with performers such as acrobats and animals such as elephants
   and horses that usually takes place in a large tent. Many circuses travel
   from town to town.

79 **leather** (page 55)
   a strong material made from animal skin that is used for making shoes,
   clothes, bags, etc.

80 **distracting** (page 59)
   stopping you from concentrating on something

81 **peasant** (page 61)
   someone who works on another person's farm or on their own small
   farm. This word is used mainly about people in poor countries or
   people in history.

82 **steel** (page 64)

a strong metal made from a mixture of iron and *carbon* – a chemical element that is found in all living things

83 **reform** (page 65)

a change that is intended to correct a situation that is wrong or unfair, or make a system work more effectively

84 **superpower** (page 69)

a country that has great military, economic and political power

85 **gymnast** (page 70)

someone who does *gymnastics* – a sport involving difficult physical exercises designed to increase your strength and ability to bend and balance – especially someone who takes part in competitions

86 **metro** (page 70)

an underground railway system in a city. The usual British English word for the underground railway system in London is *the tube*. The American word is *subway*.

87 **terminal** (page 70)

a large building at an airport where passengers arrive and leave

88 **satellite** (page 74)

an object that is sent into space to travel round the Earth in order to receive and send information

Useful Phrases

took control – *to take control of something* (page 6)
to get the power to make decisions about what happens in a place or situation

made up of – *to be made up of something* (page 13)
to be combined together to form something larger or more complicated

could not get enough of – *can't get enough of something* (page 22)
to like something very much and want a lot of it

making sure – *to make sure (that)* (page 32)
to take the action necessary to be sure that something will happen or be done

the basis of – *to be the basis of something* (page 33)
to be the important ideas, facts or actions from which something develops

side by side (page 35)
used for talking about two or more things that are very different but that exist together in the same place or are used for the same thing

had something to do with – *to have / be something to do with something* (page 42)
used for saying that something is related to something else, especially when you do not know how or do not give the exact details

sorry for – *to be / feel sorry for someone* (page 51)
to feel sympathy for someone because they are in a difficult or unpleasant situation

a must – *to be a must* (page 54)
to be something that you definitely need in a particular situation

wait and see – *to wait and see* (page 73)
to wait until you find out what happens in the future

Glossary and Useful Phrases definitions adapted from the Macmillan English Dictionary *2ⁿᵈ Edition*
© *Macmillan Publishers Limited 2007* www.macmillandictionary.com

Exercises

Welcome to China

Which of these things does *Welcome to China* talk about? Tick the boxes.

geography ✓   language ☐
sport ☐   computers ☐
school life ☐   religion ☐
economy ☐   history ☐

Background Information

Complete the gaps. Use each word in the box once.

> dynasty   economies   emperors   ethnic   famous   flag
> landscapes   Mandarin   Mao Zedong   ~~third~~

1 China is the _____ *third* _____ biggest country in the world.

2 Most people in China speak _____ .

3 Some _____ minorities speak other languages.

4 China is a big country and there are many different _____ .

5 The Great Wall of China is very _____ .

6 For nearly four thousand years, China was ruled by _____ .

7 In 1911, the last _____ ended and China became a Republic.

8 _____ and the Communist party took control of the country in 1949.

9 Since the end of the twentieth century, China has become one of the most important _____ in the world.

10 There are five yellow stars on the red _____ of China.

Contents

Write the correct chapter number next to each topic in the book.

Recent history	☐	Karaoke	☐
Geography	*1*	The Dragon Boat Festival	☐
China in the future	☐	Kung fu	☐
Calligraphy	☐	Ancient history	☐
Food	☐	Herbal medicine	☐

Reading Comprehension

Read the statements about China. Choose T (True) or F (False).

1 The Yangtze is called 'the Mother River' by people in China. T / **(F)**

2 Most of the population of China belong to the Han group. T / F

3 Sima Qian wrote the first history of China during the Han dynasty. T / F

4 During the Tang dynasty China was ruled by a woman. T / F

5 Calligraphy artists never write on paper. T / F

6 'Wuxia' is a type of martial art. T / F

7 Traditional Chinese Medicine is no longer used in hospitals. T / F

8 Chinese New Year is on 1st January every year. T / F

9 Colours are used in the Peking Opera to show the type of character. T / F

10 Sun Yat-sen became the first president of China in 1911. T / F

11 Deng Xiaoping became General Secretary after Mao Zedong died. T / F

12 The World Expo took place in Beijing in 2010. T / F

Vocabulary: Geography

Complete the gaps. Use each word from the box once.

> ~~border~~   climates   desert   fertile   flow   grasslands
> humid   lowlands   plateau   valleys

1 Mount Everest, the highest mountain in the world, is on the China–Nepal .... *border* ....

2 Tibet, in the south-west of the country, is a high .... and is often called the 'roof of the world'.

3 In the centre and south of China the summers can be long, hot and

....

4 There are still some wild camels in the Taklamakan ...., but they are disappearing fast.

5 Both the Yangtze and the Yellow river .... into the East China Sea.

6 The land along the Yangtze river is very .... and lots of food is grown there.

7 The north-central part of China was once covered in .... and forests, but most of those have now disappeared.

8 The area of Hubei province is famous for its deep .... and high mountains.

9 The .... in the south-east of China are wet and warm all year long.

10 China is such a large country that it has many different ...., from the cold winters in the north to the very long, hot summers in central China.

Vocabulary: Food

Choose the correct word to complete the sentences.

1 For lunch Chinese people usually have several (**dishes**) / **foods** of vegetables, meat and fish to choose from.

2 Traditional **cafes** / **teahouses** are disappearing in China as young people want to go to more western-style places.

3 The Chinese believe that a meal should have a good **balance** / **harmony** of food.

4 Each region in China has its own **cuisine** / **meals**. These often have different flavours as well as different dishes.

5 The food in Sichuan is famous for being hot and **bitter** / **spicy** and has lots of garlic, ginger and chilli peppers in it.

6 *Kuaizi*, or **chopsticks** / **knives**, are used for eating food most of the time.

7 The most common types of **cuisine** / **tea** are green, black and *oolong*.

8 Many people like to drink green tea because it has a fresh **taste** / **harmony** and a sweet smell.

Vocabulary: Anagrams

Write the letters in the correct order to make words which match the definitions.

1	POREMER	*emperor*	a man who rules an empire
2	KNOM		a man who lives in a religious community and lives by the rules of a religion
3	STAMER		a famous artist
4	TAPANES		someone who works on another person's farm or on their own small farm
5	THOS		someone who invites people to a meal or a party, or to stay in their home
6	SNAGTMY		someone who does gymnastics, especially someone who takes part in competitions
7	BRITEHALS		someone who grows, sells or prepares herbs – plants used as medicine
8	GEOLOCHRAITS		someone who studies archeology

Useful Phrases

Match the phrase beginnings (1–7) to the phrase endings (a–g) to make a phrase from the text.

1	cannot get		**a**	control
2	wait		**b**	enough
3	have something		**c**	sure
4	take		**d**	and see
5	side		**e**	for
6	sorry		**f**	by side
7	make		**g**	to do with

Match the phrases to their definitions.

1 to like something very much and want a lot of it ___1___

2 to take action to be certain something will happen ....

3 to feel sympathy for someone because they are in a difficult or unpleasant situation ....

4 to wait until you find out what happens in the future ....

5 to get the power to do something and make decisions ....

6 used for talking about two things or more that are very different but exist together in the same place or are used for the same thing ....

7 when something is related to something else, especially when you don't know the exact details ....

Grammar: Tenses

Complete the sentences with the correct form of the verbs in brackets.

1 China _____*covers*_____ (cover) a large geographical area so it is a country with many different landscapes.

2 There are still some wild camels in the Taklamakan Desert but they _____ (disappear) fast.

3 People _____ (live) on the land along the Yangtze for thousands of years.

4 The first emperor, Qin Shihuang, _____ (build) a wall along the northern border of his empire.

5 The Ming emperors _____ (rule) for almost three hundred years before they were conquered by the Manchus.

6 The Buddhist monks at Shaolin Temple _____ (be) famous for their fighting style – Shaolin kung fu.

7 The Chinese _____ (knew) for thousands of years that plants are good for treating diseases.

8 Chinese New Year _____ (finish) with the Festival of Lanterns on the 15th day after the new moon.

9 Chinese people enjoy _____ (have) meals together with their families and friends.

10 Peking Opera _____ (include) acrobatics and martial arts as well as music, drama and singing.

11 Sun Yat-sen studied medicine in Hong Kong. But while he _____ (study), he became a revolutionary.

12 In the future, China _____ (play) an important part in the world's future.

Grammar: Active or passive?

Choose the correct verb form, active or passive, to complete the sentences.

1 The Loess Plateau gets its name from the yellow soil which **finds** / (**is found**) there.

2 The country **divided** / **is divided** into twenty-two provinces, four municipalities, five Autonomous Regions and two Special Administrative Regions.

3 The written words, or characters, in Chinese **based on** / **are based on** simple drawings.

4 In 1974 archeologists **discovered** / **were discovered** a terracotta army buried with the first emperor, Qin Shihuang.

5 During the Han dynasty, paper, printing and water clocks **all invented** / **were all invented**.

6 In AD 618 a government official, Li Yuan, **killed** / **was killed** the last emperor of the Sui dynasty and started the mighty Tang dynasty.

7 Song Dong is one of China's most famous artists. One of his works, *Eating the City*, **made** / **is made** of food.

8 The first book on Chinese traditional medicine **probably wrote** / **was probably written** in the second century BC.

9 When Chinese people want to entertain guests they often **hold** / **are held** banquets in big restaurants.

10 Chopsticks **usually made** / **are usually made** of bamboo and are used just once.

Grammar: Adjective forms

Complete the sentences with the correct form of the adjectives.

1 Mount Everest is the .... mountain in the world.
   a high   **b** higher   (**c** highest)

2 China has many different climates and temperatures can get as .... as -41 degrees centigrade in some places.
   a low   **b** lower   **c** lowest

3 The third _____ river in China is the Pearl River, which flows into the South China Sea.

    a long   **b** longer   **c** longest

4 During the Han dynasty, trade became _____ because of the Silk Road.

    a as easy   **b** easier   **c** easiest

5 During the Song dynasty, China was probably the _____ country in the world.

    a rich   **b** richer   **c** richest

6 During the second half of the nineteenth century, the Qing dynasty became _____ than ever before and there were many problems in the country.

    a weak   **b** weaker   **c** weakest

7 During the sixteenth century, Chinese porcelain was so _____ that it became known as 'white gold'.

    a expensive   **b** more expensive   **c** most expensive

8 *Go* is probably the _____ board game in the world.

    a old   **b** older   **c** oldest

Pronunciation: Sounds

Are the underlined sounds the same or different?

1	lo<u>ng</u>	<u>o</u>ld	same / (different)
2	<u>ch</u>opsticks	te<u>ch</u>nique	same / different
3	revolu<u>ti</u>on	offi<u>ci</u>al	same / different
4	bamb<u>oo</u>	metr<u>o</u>	same / different
5	for<u>c</u>e	<u>s</u>orrow	same / different
6	<u>c</u>ircus	<u>c</u>onquered	same / different

Macmillan Education
4 Crinan Street
London N1 9XW
A division of Macmillan Publishers Limited
Companies and representatives throughout the
world

ISBN 978-0-230-46036-2
ISBN 978-0-230-46040-9 (with CD edition)

Text, design and illustration © Macmillan
Publishers Limited 2014
Written by Jennifer Gascoigne
The author has asserted her right to be identified
as the author of this work in accordance with the
Copyright, Designs and Patents Act 1988.

First published 2014

Designed by Carolyn Gibson
Map by Peter Harper
Cover photographs by Corbis/Martin Puddy (r),
Corbis/Travelpix Collection (tl), Getty Images/
The Image Bank (bl).
Picture research by Sally Cole, Perseverance
Works Limited

The author and publishers would like to thank
the following for permission to reproduce their
photographs:
Alamy/P.Bolotov p34, Alamy/E.Elisseeva p33,
Alamy/L.Linwei p64, Alamy/C.Taylor p19;
Corbis/T.Bognar p16, Corbis/C.Boisvieux p28,
Corbis/Christies Images pp23(mr), 27, Corbis/
Concord Productions Inc./Golden Harvest
Company/Sunset Boulevard p31, Corbis/D.
Conger p10, Corbis/Feature China p74, Corbis/J.
Guariglia p25(b), Corbis/Heritage Images p23(mr),
Corbis/R.Jack p52, Corbis/S.Hing-Keung p48,
Corbis/D.Lehman p15, Corbis/Maps.com pp4, 5,
Corbis/Metaxas p47, Corbis/Minden Pictures p9,
Corbis/Radius Images p43, Corbis/Reuters pp50,
53, Corbis/K.Su p8, Corbis/Y.Lu/Viewstock p22,
Corbis/Li Ziheng/Xinhua Press p57; **Getty Images**/
AFP pp12, 60, 63, Getty Images/Blend Images p37,
Getty Images/Dorling Kindersley p36(ml), Getty
Images/Getty Images Entertainment p55, Getty
Images/Flickr p39, Getty Images/FoodPix p38,
Getty Images/Gallo Images p45, Getty Images/
Gamma-Rapho p30, Getty Images/Photolibrary
pp36(tl), 36(bl), 67, Getty Images/Iconica p58,
Getty Images/The Image Bank pp44, 49, Getty
Images/Riser p70, Getty Images/Tao Images p69,
Getty Images/Taxi p25(tl), Getty Images/Universal
Images Group p61, Getty Images/Wire Image p59;
ImageSource p72; **Macmillan** lion statue inset on
all inside pages; **Photodisc** p22(frame); **Pictures
from History**/D.Henley p21; **Plainpicture**/Axiom
p71; **Superstock** p6(bl); **Werner Foreman Archive**/
Idemitsu Museum of Arts, Tokyo p23(tr).

These materials may contain links for third party
websites. We have no control over, and are not
responsible for, the contents of such third party
websites. Please use care when accessing them.

Although we have tried to trace and contact
copyright holders before publication, in some
cases this has not been possible. If contacted we
will be pleased to rectify any errors or omissions
at the earliest opportunity.

Printed and bound in Thailand

without CD edition

2019	2018	2017	2016	2015	2014
10	9	8	7	6	5	4	3	2	1

with CD edition

2019	2018	2017	2016	2015	2014
10	9	8	7	6	5	4	3	2	1